Joshua King Ingalls

Reminiscences of an Octogenarian in the Fields of Industrial and

Social Reform

Joshua King Ingalls

Reminiscences of an Octogenarian in the Fields of Industrial and Social Reform

ISBN/EAN: 9783337295660

Printed in Europe, USA, Canada, Australia, Japan

Cover: Foto ©Suzi / pixelio.de

More available books at **www.hansebooks.com**

REMINISCENCES OF AN OCTOGENARIAN

IN THE FIELDS OF

INDUSTRIAL AND SOCIAL REFORM.

BY JOSHUA KING INGALLS,

Author of "Social Wealth," "Economic Equities," "Land and Labor," "Work and Wealth," Etc.

NEW YORK,
M. L. HOLBROOK & CO.

LONDON,
L. N. FOWLER & CO.

ELMIRA, N. Y.
GAZETTE COMPANY, PRINTERS AND PUBLISHERS,
1897.

"WHERE INDUSTRY 'IS NOT THERE CAN BE NEITHER HONESTY TOWARDS MEN NOR WORSHIP OF THE INFINITE WORKER."   J. H. HUNT.

PREFACE.

These Reminiscences, which largely refer to parties no longer dwellers of our sphere, are mainly the personal recollections of the author, who has never kept any regular diary. Where periodicals and books have been referred to, the memory has been relieved; but otherwise, it has been wholly relied upon. The motive leading to their publication, has been the request of friends, to have them put in readable form; but in addition to that, there are certain ideas I desired to put before the world in as familiar a form as possible.

I regard as essential to Social advancement, first: The apportionment of the land so as to allow no one to be deprived of its use, who is able and willing to utilize it.

Second: The recognition of the principle of joint-ownership in all increase from joint labor.

Third: Equal Freedom in the choice of occupation and association.

The trend of thought as these pages will show, has been towards a broader liberty in the pursuit of knowledge, and of every aim in life which does not invade the equal rights of others.

Of the ideas I have arrived at in respect to rent, interest, and profit as to their origin, and double meaning as they refer to increase under equity and freedom, and to the same increase under monopoly and subjection, I am not sufficiently well read to aver that they are wholly new; but they are original with me, as far as that term applies to ordinary composition.

For the statement of views on government and on all other Social matters, I have only to say that they are sincerely held and will be abandoned whenever the opposite or a more satisfactorily medium shall be made to appear rational.

I am under obligation to many minds with which I have come in contact through books, periodicals, and personal acquaintance, which cannot be referred to here. Carlyle, Emerson and Spencer, have been my favorite authors. I remember that Combe's Constitution of Man, Vestiges of Creation, and other books of that period greatly stimulated my mental activites. But through life, I have endeavored to think for myself.

I think I may claim to have made some novel contributions to Economic Science, to wit: The nature and origin of profit, interest and rent. That they are one in character, and are divisible into economic and monopolistic according to the division made to labor, and the capture through legal privilege by landlord, banker, or holder of plant and stock:

That money is also duplicate; legal and commercial.

That it is legal money, not the commercial, which begets, inflation and contraction, and causes panics and business depressions.

That it is not the balances of commerce, but the adjustments of indebtedness or rather the payment of interest on funded debts, which produces the disasters, the compulsory idleness, and distress of those who labor.

That permanent debts or dominion of land, have no relation to production or exchange, except that they are legally made to form a lien on the products of industry without any equitable claim.

That Value, or rather Price, is determined by three Ratios of Utility, invariable, of Service, stable, and of Demand and Supply, variable; the ratio of service being affected by voluntary and involuntary Status and by free or obstructed opportunity; the ratio of supply and demand being widely varied by an open market, or by exclusive privilege to forestall and monopolize it.

That Contracts, as legally interpreted, are used for the purpose of excluding equity in adjustment; and however they may bind the parties thereto, cannot bind, rightfully, courts, juries or comrades to waive a rigid inquiry into what is just or unjust in their provisions, before attempting to enforce them.

For a concise and clear statement of this principle I acknowledge my indebtedness to George E. Macdonald: I should also credit Liberty and its many writers, for clear and comprehensive views of equal freedom: and I would here render a tribute to my late companion in life, Olive H. Fraser Ingalls, for her constant sympathy and encouragement in my investigations of Social and indutsrial problems, and for actual assistance in giving expression to important truths.   J. K. I.

Glenora, July 1, 1897.

ERRATA.

Page 37, 13th line from bottom por prendo read pseudo.

Page 56, top line, transpose with which.

Page 108, 15th line from top, for untouched read touched.

Page 131, 10th line from bottom, for but, read by.

Page 161, line 14 from top, omit been.

Page 166, line 12, for are read and. Omit lines 17 and 18 and addition of true, conjugal love.

Page 169, top line, for loans, read laws.

Page 177, omit last sentence at bottom.

Page 178, omit first two lines at top.

INDEX.

J. K. INGALLS.

REMINISCENCES.

CHAPTER I.

In a secluded spot of the town of Swansea, Bristol Co., in the State of Massachusetts, on the 21st day of July 1816, the writer first saw the light. His birth stands thus recorded in the town clerk's office.

Between the towns of Dighton and Rehoboth, extends a district a mile wide and two miles long; at one time known as "the two mile purchase" which had been awarded to Swansea, under circumstances which are variously stated in colonial tradition. Nearly in the centre of this tract, remote from any public road, and partly surrounded by marshy forests, were two farms. At the beginning of this century, one was owned by Elkanah Ingalls, the father of the writer, and the other by Joseph Lewis, our only near neighbor. Our next neighbors were a half mile away through the woods, and only two other families within a mile. Our school-house, where, outside of home-teaching, I received my principal early education, was about a mile away, and adjoined the Dighton line. Our school was made up in nearly equal proportions from the parts of the districts of two towns, which held separate school-meetings, and agreed upon the hiring a common teacher, and other matters of detail for the school. My recollection goes back for more than seventy-five years, to the time when my father was yet living, but who died when I was four years of age. The first impression I remember, that things needed reforming occurred when I was about five years of age. It was the second season of going to school. I had not yet learned my letters, mainly because I could see no use in trying to repeat from memory the names given to certain characters contained in the alphabet. I remember with great distinctness of my mother's visit to the school one day, and of my mortification when the teacher told her that I was a very backward child, and she had begun to despair of ever being able to teach me my letters. Then my mother quietly asked her if she would not begin to teach me words, and the use and sound of letters in them? At first, this was strenously objected to. "It would be quite unusual," the teacher said. But my mother still urged it, and intimated that the teacher need not spend more time than she usually gave in teaching the letters. She began to show me the relation of letters to words, and words to each other. To her astonishment I manifested an immediate interest in identifying the letters, and in two weeks time I was reading readily, and correctly short sentences in one and two syllables. In a few years I was only second in spelling, and at nine years of age took the coveted certificate at close of school, for being at the head of the spelling-class, although there were several scholars grown to manhood, and womanhood in the class. In this manner at the early age of five years, I had practical illustration, that authority and established methods of teaching were subject to question, and my mind was thus early directed to original thinking, and the investigation by myself, of any and all questions which became subjects of discussion. In a matter of similar character, I was greatly put back by faults in my early instruction. As soon as a slate was allowed me in school, as in other children, the desire to draw was awakened. This was strictly prohibited by "the rules of the school," and many a scene between teacher and scholar, is remembered, when deliquency was discovered in that respect. No teaching would ever have made me an artist, probably; but in maturer life, a little knowledge of drawing would have been of vast benefit to me, saving an immense amount of tiresome labor and mortification when the necessities of my business as inventor, and constructor required.it.

Our neighborhood was not an educated one, nor refined in the popular sense; but much kind feeling, and friendly service were exercised. There was a marked toleration of thought among the different religious societies and political parties, for those times, as compared with other localities. Amid these peaceful and quiet scenes I lived till in my fifteenth year, the necessity of doing something for self-support led me to seek employment in what is now, the City of Providence, and which about half a century since, abandoned the primitive town-meeting, for a Mayor, Aldermen and Council. To those days of childhood and youth, my mind is ever drawn with mingled emotions of pleasure and sadness. In imagination I see again the green fields, the dim woods, the streams and ponds, and even the swamps impassable to pedestrians except in winter frost and summer drowth, the immense boulders, which to my childish imagination seemed mountains, but which at an early age I learned to climb, and so enjoy the wilder scene given from the elevation. I hear again, the singing of the sparrow, the thrush, and bobolink, and see the white birches, we children climbed so oft, to enjoy the sensation of the descent, bending them with our weight till we could reach the ground. This was often at the peril of being suspended too high in mid air to safely let go. All these things seem fresh in my memory, as the occurrences of yesterday, though more than three score years have flown, since these enjoyments were experienced in the simple and healthful sport.

It was our custom to climb the tree as near the top as possible, and clutch it with both hands, then throw the body clear to one side, and then, if we were not able to descend near enough to the ground to reach it safely, run one hand over the other, until the flexibility of the extreme end would secure a sufficient depression. In cases of unusual resistance a comrade would climb upon the same tree and by his additional weight bring the suspended one safely to earth.

Running, wrestling, playing various games, requiring speed and shrewdness, gave us all the advantages of the modern gymnasium, to say nothing of chopping wood and engaging in the work of the farm and such handicrafts as were common in the country.

I have little doubt that my own development of muscle in the arms and chest was due in a considerable degree to those early sports and outdoor exercises which were always for "the fun of the thing" and never for a pecuniary reward or the wining of a prize. That prize money or gate money is necessary in any healthful sport, is the mere subterfuge of greed and the gambling habit. There is no more necessity for it as an inducement to the attainment of perfectibility in action than there is justification for the brutal maiming of a fellow being, to prove which of two well trained men can strike the hardest blow, or sustain the greatest and longest continual fatigue. Blows can be measured accurately to an ounce as to their effectiveness, and endurance can be as accurately determined, by proper contrivances; whereas, pugilism often turns, as contended by many in the late prize fights, on a mere chance hit or "scratch shot." The gambling mania debauches every subject to which it attaches. Some one has said that the worst use you can put a man to is to hang him; but much depends on the worth of the individual. To take so much pains to train a man and bring him into an excellent physical condition and then batter him to pieces, is as devoid of economic as of ethical justification.

Then there was the district school, (which I, myself taught at eighteen), the emulation in the spelling-school contests, the noonings and recesses, with mornings before and evenings after school; sliding on the ice—for the luxury of skates was scarcely known to us—the ice bending when thaws occurred, not really perilous, the ponds being shallow, but in which many of us were often thoroughly wet, eliciting a stern rebuke from our teacher and parents, when discovered. Later came the singing-school, the husking frolic, the rural parties of the young, with such plays as were tolerated; but never dancing, as this with cards was strictly prohibited.

The religious meetings must not be forgotten. The Baptist "meeting house," the only one within several miles of us, was under a cloud, through division, and the falling away of the pastor, who after many years of service succumbed at last to the bottle. We were early visited by the Methodists, and preachers of other sects; our school house being our place of worship, our meetings being usually held on week-day evenings, and only occasionally upon Sunday.

At an early age, I became deeply interested in religious questions; but when I manifested a desire to identify myself with the religious revival proceeding when I was nine years of age, I was told I was too young. Thus early my eyes began to open to the inconsistencies, not to say the insincerity of professors of religion. But I kept on thinking nevertheless; and when the excitement passed away, and the converts many of them became back-sliders, as they used to be called, I drew the conclusion that if their religion made them as happy as was claimed, it was strange that they did not hold on to it longer. The discussion of doctrines next drew my attention, and I began to speculate as to the reasonableness of the doctrine of the trinity, vicarious atonement and so forth, which I concluded should be made to appear reasonable, if true.

It was but a short time before, that the believers calling themselves Christians, but who were called by their opposers "Smithites," began to disturb the orthodoxy of the time, and to create division, particularly among the Baptists. A number had left the church to which my father had belonged, and of which my mother, and an elder brother remained members, long after his decease. Among the seceders, was a cousin of my mother, Elder George Kelton, whose son, George N. Kelton, became a preacher of the new denomination, and whose ministry extended through a full half century, mainly I think in New York: in Columbia, Yates and other counties in the western part of the State.

Thus early in life I was brought face to face with the fact that sectarian profession had little to do with real character and that the best people could widely differ in their religious faith. Later, I learned that true merit depended in no way upon profession of any kind, but upon the growth of the inherited and attained principle of wisdom in the individual. Comparing the professors of the newer faith with those of the old, I came to the conclusion that individual character, far oftener affects religious opinions than opinions affect character, for the piety and religious observances are often determined by the results of inheritance or early instruction. In New England the extension of the more liberal faith was largely due to the preaching and writings of Elias Smith, a self-taught man of limited acquirements, but of much vigor, and originality of thought. In the early part of this century, he started their first denominational newspaper "The Watchman," which is still published, I believe. He had already made a success of it, when at a Convention of the "Elders," it was requested that he should make it the organ of their order, subject to their supervision and control. This, he peremptorily refused to do, or submit in any way to a censorship. He offered however to sell his plant and good will on terms, which they accepted. His name is now seldom mentioned by their preachers, and to ministers, as well as laymen seems a name unknown.

They wished to make their movement embrace all the "reason of Harvard, with all the fire of Andover," and did not want anything uttered which would imperil their relation with either side. This attitude they have apparently maintained to the present time, working with the orthodox in evangelical revival measures, while rejecting the doctrine of vicarious atonement, the main justification of such work, and while affiliating in more liberal things with the Unitarians and Universalists.

Mr. Smith afterwards became a physician, a "steam doctor," or "Thomsonian," as these practitioners were afterwards called, and did much by his ever ready wit, and versatile pen to make "blood letting" and "calomel" unpopular. He was the father of Matthew Hale Smith, a very eccentric but talented preacher, who changed many times from his parent's faith, to Universalism,—then to Orthodoxy, making at each change a telling point of the renunciation of the one, for the other. I last knew of him, as a brusque lawyer in the city of New York.

CHAPTER II.

As already stated, at the age of fifteen, I went to Providence, and obtained a place in the Bleaching and Callender works. I boarded with a family which came from our neighborhood, and whose members attended the Methodist Church in Chestnut Street. I was induced to attend the Sunday School, and was given a class to teach. It was while trying to make plain to young minds, the lessons in the "Union" question books, that I first became impressed with the absurdity of the claims put forth for the inerrancy of the Bible, and of the contradictory character of the tenets of the church generally. In the school, and during the sermons, which I weekly listened to, I gradually became a chronic critic of everything I heard or read upon the subject of religion. The bias of my early training constantly sought to assert itself by the suggestion that such attitude of mind was improper if not wicked. For several years this tendency to criticism increased; and naturally disposed me to argument. I often astonished, and no doubt pained my best friends by suggesting subjects of doubt and misgiving as to the truth of their beliefs.

I remember that while teaching my class, the pastor came to me one day, and sought to ascertain my method of instruction. I explained that the books gave, or suggested the answers, and that it was merely necessary to see that the children recited these verbal answers. He seemed satisfied, but said that I should not confine myself wholly to the printed questions; but should ask others, and that he wished I would question the children as to their home-teaching: whether they had family prayers, grace said at meals, reading of the Scriptures, and so forth. As I was beginning to doubt on general principles, the utility of these formalities, being acquainted with the views of the Friends or Quakers, and as I naturally revolted at playing the part of spy on the private home, I was at a loss what to say to him, but calling to mind that his son, a bright boy of eight or nine years was in my class, I gave consent, though not without a mental reservation. So, when the lesson was through, and the time of closing had not arrived, I called the boy to me, and quietly put the questions to him. And really I was not surprised that every one was answered in the negative.

It was about this time, I began to be interested in political affairs. Gen. Jackson was entering on his second term as President, and the questions of the Tariff, of Nullification, and of the United States Bank (Biddle's) created great excitement among the people. But while my untrained thought was mainly in approval of the General's course it was his attitude in regard to the public lands, and his proposition to hold them simply as a trust for the actual settlers, and to abandon the idea of deriving a revenue from them, which completely won my heart.

The contrary policy had been followed from the formation of our Government. Hamilton, the first Secretary of our Treasury, had thought to build up a landed aristocracy upon that basis, and to lay off the national debt, by sale of these lands, to native and to foreign purchasers, who wished to establish large estates. He ruled that only those who could purchase a mile square could deal directly with the Government, and that the hardy pioneers who were to settle and improve these lands, must hire or purchase of forestallers, unless they were prepared to buy six hundred and forty acres (640), requiring eight hundred dollars ($800) to be invested in land at the start; a sum, it is safe to say, scarcely one in one hundred of those possessed, who sought to better their condition, by emigration. This policy was not changed until the administration of Thos. Jefferson and mainly through the persistent exertions of Gen. Wm. H. Harrison, at that time delegate in Congress from the North-west Territory. As former governor of that Territory he had seen the direful effects of Hamilton's system of reducing the pioneers to the dependent condition of tenants or of debtors to speculators, who stood between them and the soil, through favor of the laws, or of those who administered them. I did not at that time apprehend the true nature of land ownership, that of occupation and use; but the injustice of giving the public heritage to a privileged class to perpetuate the dependency of the workers, and for purposes of wild speculation was apparent, and I could but feel that the old General was the true friend of the industrious poor, and of the whole people.

At this time too, there was great activity among the workingmen, and strikes were organized in many cities simultaneously to obtain the ten hour system. The bosses, and manufacturers combined against it. It was fruitless or nearly so. Seth Luther, of Rhode Island, Dr. Douglas of Connecticut, and ex-Rev. Jacob Frieze were among the leading spirits of the movement. The establishment in which I worked, of its own motion, after the strike had failed, extended the hour of dinner from three quarters to one hour, and reduced the length of the day in summer to seven o'clock instead of sunset. Some other trades adopted eleven hours. I felt thus early a deep interest in the labor question, and my sympathies were enlisted upon the side of the workers. The question of manhood suffrage was also connected with the movement in Rhode Island. At that time only owners of real estate, and their eldest sons were entitled to vote. This latter question continued to be agitated after the ten hour question was allowed to slumber, culminating in 1841 in the Dorr Rebellion.

It was impossible that I should have failed to be stimulated by these occurrences, to the consideration of the nature of government, and the effect of legislation generally on the condition of the working people.

When scarcely in my teens, I had heard my school teacher explain the operation of the interest problem, and that it proceeded by geometrical progression, since by using the money paid as interest, and again investing it, it fulfilled the conditions of a duplicate ratio. I had learned enough of arithmetic to know what that meant, and was astounded to find that neither my teacher, nor any of the pupils had the least conception of its enormity and injustice. In thinking upon the subject of labor and capital at the period (of agitation) previously referred to, I imagined I had discovered the cause of the disadvantage in which the former stood to the latter; and seeing the stupendous power of wealth accumulated on the one hand, and the increasing dependence of the worker upon the other, thought the solution reached, and that it was only necessary to inaugurate a reform, to which all the force of morals, and of religion would be given, to redress the wrongs of labor, and give to all the just fruits of their toil. It seemed an easy thing to do to show the workingmen, and religious and moral people, that interest was derived from the profits which capital obtained from the production of labor, and that to remedy the ills of the toilers, it was only necessary to apply the principle of anti-usury so clearly maintained by the Bible, and by the old moralists, to settle the labor problem, and introduce the millenium, when "distributive justice should pervade the industrial world." After sixty years of endeavor, I have found how difficult it is to induce the respectably pious, and exemplary moral to think, much less act, on the lines of industrial reform. With youthful expectation, I began to talk to working men on the subject, but found none who could understand me. Their leaders told me, it would not do to introduce such subjects. I sought to enlist religious people in it, but with no better success. Clergymen who should have known better, and possibly did, told me that the Scripture denunciations against usury meant illegal, not lawful interest. It was quite ten years, before I found a single individual who expressed sympathy with my view, or would give serious consideration to the subject.

CHAPTER III.

In 1833, I was apprenticed to Messrs. James Eames & Co., of Providence to learn the trade of sheet metal worker. I here came in contact with more cultivated people, than hitherto. Mr. Eames' son, James, was preparing for college. He afterwards studied for orders in the Episcopal Church, and became a Doctor of Divinity. Another son, Henry, was in later years a Member of Congress. Their clerk was Amos C. Barstow, a young man of talent, who identified himself with the Temperance, and other reforms, and was ultimately made Mayor of the City. On entering this establishment, I was given a ticket entitling me to get books from the Mechanics and Apprentices' Library. This would have been of more value to me, if I had been able to make judicious selections; but having previously read some books of romance, the love of fiction was indulged to the neglect of more solid reading. However, the reading of Scott, Cooper, Irving, and other English classics, gave me a general idea of the times and places they described, a taste for good English, and a better knowledge of history, than the more trashy literature would have done.

The cause of Temperance, then in its incipiency, had been frequently discussed in our rural neighborhood; but with no great favor. It interfered with the habits of the people, and was looked upon, by many as an insidious scheme to undermine liberty of thought and action. The drinking of New England Rum was a common thing. Every family kept it in the house, and few farmers thought they could get through the heavy farm work in hot weather, or the winter's work in the cold, without constant resort to this popular stimulant. Both at weddings, and at funerals as well as at all social gatherings, it was freely used; but seldom to the extent of drunkenness.

In the winter of 1830, the wife of a neighbor died. He was a constant drinker, but always kept upright, and to appearance sober. It was in the midst of an unusual snow-fall, and no teams were able to get out. Neighboring women came to the house as they best could, to assist, and thought that the usual dinner and refreshments should be served. Whatever was obtained, was brought on foot over the drifted snow, from a store more than two miles away. The women suggested that they should have a little tea, as they could find none in the house. The man replied that he did not like to burden the young man who was to go for them, as he had already given him orders for more than he could well bring, under the circumstances, and as the two gallon jugs of "liquor which must be had," were about all he ought to bring. I refer to this condition of things simply to emphasize the progress, which the Temperance Reform has made in the last sixty-five years. The cause of Temperance had all these conditions, habits and prejudices to contend with. I was too young when I left the country to have such prejudices exert a lasting influence on me.

Mr. Eames, his partner, and Mr. Barstow, were advocates of Temperance, as abstinence from distilled liquors only was termed. They required me to take the pledge which I felt compelled to do, though with a little reluctance. I do not remember attending any temperance meetings, or feeling any particular interest in the question, till about a year after signing the pledge. Then Sylvester Graham was giving lectures on Vegetarianism, and also lectures to young men. Mr. Barstow invited me to attend some of them. The earnest and eloquent words of the Lecturer, his fine address and engaging manners enlisted a deep interest in the man and his theme. It might have occurred to me, that his enthusiasm bordered on fanaticism, but I could not avoid the conclusion that there was abundant need of reform in the field he had chosen. It was then I resolved that total abstinence from all intoxicants was to be my rule in life. And this private resolution I was enabled to maintain for thirty years. Since then, as age crept on occasional stimulants have been employed, but their use has never become a habit with me. For the same length of time, I used no tea or coffee, and at times have used no animal food; but in this, I have found more difficulty, since in this respect, more depends on those, with whom one lives. If a family or community were united on the question, I am satisfied there would be little inconvenience in doing without flesh diet.

Be this as it may, Sylvester Graham, the innovator, and reformer is most certainly entitled to the respect and gratitude of mankind. His name has been immortalized, by being joined to unbolted flour and the bread made from it; but posterity can hardly appreciate the good he did, in arousing the attention of people to the importance of understanding how to correct the evils of sexual excess, springing from ignorance, and weakness of purpose. Everything of this nature was previously scrupulously tabooed in the family, and in society. Of the origin of life, and the physiology of sex, all was left to be learned surreptitiously by children, and from ignorant, and already corrupted associates. Laws against obscene literature, prints and so forth, have availed nothing, and never will against ignorance, and deception, and the false accounting for the facts of life, by parents and which can only for a very brief period deceive the dullest child. It is not a question for ill-digested, and ill-enforced laws, but of early education and development of self-respect, and self-control in the child which confronts parents, if they desire their children to grow up in intelligence and virtue.

To the influence of my associates in the shop, I owed much. There were several men, young and old, who were above the ordinary standard. A journeyman, by the name of Sargent, was well educated, and of highly refined nature and inclined to liberal views in religion. His precepts, and example were of great value to me, as was also that of one or two others. Samuel A. Briggs was an elder apprentice, who always stimulated my mental activities, though tending to the sardonic in humor, and the cynical in philosophy. Anson G. Lewis was less cultured, but of a vigorous tone in thought, he was exact and upright, although occasionally led to excess in drink. I have not met in after life, either of these parties, but their distinct individualities, deeply impressed themselves upon my mind, and are vividly distinct on the tablets of my memory, whenever I recur to those days now past, more than three score years.

My employers took more than usual interest in the intellectual, and religious improvement of their men, the apprentices, particularly. We were sent in winter to an evening school; but in which, we had little attention from the teachers. It was in this school, that I became acquainted with Edwin Eddy, who afterwards became a D. D. among the Baptists, and who with several others organized a debating society, which extended to me, and one other of our apprentices an invitation to join. It was in this, that my taste for discussion, and careful investigation manifested itself. I well remember my first essay to speak. The subject seemed plain enough, and there was much to be said, on one side at least. I arose, without any thought of difficulty, but had scarcely finished my opening sentence, when the sound of my voice quite confused, and alarmed me. The result was, "stage fright." Luckily the question had proved an interesting one, and was continued till next week. I therefore prepared by writing out, what appeared pertinent to the question and experienced no inconvenience in reading it; and I was complimented, by those who were experienced in debate.

After working at the bench, some two years or more, my left arm was burned by an explosion of some melted solder. I was unable to work for some time, and when the burn was healed, remained an invalid for many weeks. I had gone home to my mother, in Swansea, and inconsiderately accepted an invitation to teach the district school, where my limited education had been chiefly received. Yet the experience of that term was of value to me, in demonstrating the necessity of exactness in pursuing studies. I had several young men and women, older than myself, for pupils, and who were capable of reasoning upon questions, which arose in process of teaching. The school was well ordered, and the winter passed pleasantly. No corporeal punishment was employed, nor did I find difficulty in maintaining decorum, without it.

But the effect of my leaving my mechanical employment, was not advantageous to my material prosperity. Constant employment as teacher, was out of the question, unless I had been much better qualified and equipped. For a year, or more, I was without steady employment, when finally I went with Mr. James Smith of Warren, Rhode Island, to complete my trade, and with whom I remained till I was of age. He started a shop in Providence, quite near the old stand in Westminister St., and sent me to superintend it. At first it promised a success, but on the approach of the financial crisis of 1837, his limited means proved unequal to the emergency and with many others he had to succumb to the inevitable, and make an assignment to his creditors. It was during the winter of '36 and '37 that I renewed my acquaintance with the members of the earlier debating society. I do not remember whether the organization was the same; but there were many of the same persons. Messrs. Eddy. Weaver, Rounds, and a number of students of Brown University. Some of those who treated me with respect and even with deference as a debator in our meetings, would fail to recognize me in the street in my work day clothes. But I never allowed this to trouble me. I was pursuing a calling serviceable to society. It was those, in my estimation, who were living upon the labor of others, who needed to apologize for their position, however, laudible their efforts to improve their minds, and prepare themselves for future usefulness, might be. Perhaps this stimulated me also to give my leisure hours to reading and study.

In the winter of 1836 and '37, I became acquainted with John B. Gough, who afterwards made himself famous as a reformed drunkard and popular Temperance lecturer. He was learning the book binding business with a Mr. Gladding of New York City, who in the year of the great fire, had been burnt out. He removed his establishment to Bristol, R. I. in 1835, bringing young Gough with him and who soon made himself popular with the young men of Bristol. He had been a close attendant of theatres in New York, was somewhat versed in the elocution of the comic stage, naturally eloquent and a great mimic. Church temperance, had become at that time popular and Bristol was under "local option," a "no license" town. I often heard Gough speak. He held forth on Temperance, and on religious topics also; and made himself conspicuous in Methodist prayer and revival meetings. He was also a favorite among a class of young men who were not noted for their religion or temperance, at whose clubs or coteries, he gave recitations, sang comic songs and gave other exhibitions of his versatile genius. On going to Providence from Warren, I found Mr. Gough at the boarding house which I had selected. He often entertained us, of an evening, with a song or recitation or story. Sometimes serious—but usually of a comic nature. He recited "The Sailor Boy's Dream," with peculiar tragic expression, and sang. "The Cork Leg," a "Trip up to Richmond by Water," with inimitable humor and grimace.

His exit from the boarding house was serio-comic. Our landlord had hardly obeyed the Scriptural injunction to "Owe no man anything," but was running up accounts whenever he could. It was the

era of expansion. A number of creditors had adopted the plan of
"boarding it out," either directly or by proxy. Mr. Gough's employer happened to be a creditor, and was having Gough
board there in order to get his pay. This was true of
several others. Two young men and myself were paying cash every
Saturday night. That year the cows seemed to have anticipated
the period of contraction, soon to follow in the commercial world,
and had left the market bare of good butter—at least so the landlord
said. But what was short in quantity, was made up in quality, that
is strength. That which found its way to our table was of the highest rank. We complained singly and collectively; but the strength
increased. At last, at supper one evening, it proved so strong that
it got up and moved from side to side, some of it trying to run up
the ceiling, but sticking fast on the way. There was commotion in
the kitchen, and next morning an investigation was held, and several boarders were discharged, among them was the very popular
Gough, though he was really very little to blame. On inquiry it was
found that of a good half dozen who had been turned away, no one
who paid cash had been included in the number, though I fear myself
and the two friends from Warren were as culpable as any.

There was, at this time, no theatre in Providence; but a company
of quite respectable talent, had been playing in "Masonic Hall," over
the old market. After a short success some division arose in the
company, and there were not enough left to make up the necessary
parts. A number of amateurs came forward however, and entertain-
ments were continued, though I think mainly at Washington hall
on the west side. Mr. Gough and a young man by the name of Wheel-
er were the principal amateurs. Mr. Gough had taken a number of
minor characters with success and by some contingency was put forward to take the role of Sir Edmund Mortimer, in the "Iron Chest."
His personal friends rallied to his support, and there was a good
house. But considerable doubt was in the minds of his best friends
as to whether he would be equal to the character. This he seemed
to feel and the first act passed off without removing the doubt. He
obtained little applause but escaped being hissed. The second act
passed nearly in the same manner, and I could discern that the
want of appreciation was telling on him when at a turn of the dia-

logue, peculiarly suitable to his style, he elicited a slight applause: this was taken up with great spirit by his personal friends, and prolonged till nearly the whole house joined in it. From this point onward he acquitted himself like an old actor, not without some breaks and faults, but with general success.

Mr. Gough was really a "sensitive," whose success as a speaker depended mainly upon his tact of getting into sympathy with his audience. In later years I have met him but once and that was upon a steamer in the Sound. We recognized each other, and recalled the old scenes: but he had become conservative, and worldly, and seemed to take but little interest in anything but the special work of temperance reform and such religious and social questions as centered in his successful field of labor.

Not a year after my removal from Providence, the lapse of the Temperance Reformer was chronicled, and his damaging debauch made public. I think the thing was greatly exaggerated. When I last knew him, he was by no means a drunkard. I never saw him the least intoxicated. It may be true, as was circulated, that he went often from his Temperance lectures, to the saloons with his society friends and drank with them, but I never saw it manifest any marked effect upon his carriage. He would do similar things after a revival meeting: go out and meet his tony friends and joke about how he had "fooled the fanatics." But those who best understood him, only saw that it was himself he had fooled. With his sensitive, sympathetic nervous system, he actually entered into the sphere of his mental surroundings, sad or gay, temperate or intemperate, religious or irreligious, with equal zest, and with equal sincerity.

In the Washingtonian movement, it had become a fad among the reform speakers to tell the hardest stories upon themselves and this rivalry among reformed men, was responsible for many tough, as well as touching stories. Mr. Gough was not an exception to this rule and he excelled in exaggeration, as well as in vivid description of the scenes he had or had not passed through. It was unquestionably his spiritual environment at the time which made attractive his temperance and religious utterances rather than any logical deductions from moral principles, or well established premises.

I was once told by an official of the Sing Sing Prison, that during revivals of religion in the prison, converts would often draw fearful pictures of their past lives, and were most deeply affected, wnen making the wildest drafts upon their imaginations for their statements. In the words of this matter of fact, and somewhat irreverent official. "The bigger the lies, the greater the religious fervor of the narrator became." But his judgment was as wide of the mark, as that of Gou h's critics, who thought of him only as a hypocritical impostor. To correctly judge of the attitude of any mind to any subject whatever, the mental and moral atmosphere in which such mind moves must be given due consideration.

CHAPTER IV.

Upon the breaking up of the business occasioned by Mr. Smith's failure there was great difficulty in obtaining steady and remunerative employment. I went to Fall River for a while; but returned to Providence after a few months. I now became acquainted with Rev. Wm. S. Balch, pastor of the First Universalist Church. The Young Peoples' Institute, which I had joined, was held in the vestry of this Church. Mr. Balch often attended and took part in our discussions. It was here I was first introduced to him, and we were sometimes pitted in debate with each other. He invited me to his study and the use of his library, and finding that my employment was not constant, proposed that I should join a class who were studying with him. Among those I met at his house were a Mr. B. H. Davis, Mr. Wood a young student at Brown University, Zephaniah Baker and a Mr. Richards, all of whom were studying with him for the ministry. Brought in personal contact with him, and with them, religious doctrines again became subjects of thought with me, and finding the mental atmosphere so free, and more exhilerating, than it had ever been among the other sects, I was very naturally drawn into sympathy with the broader faith, more particularly as it gave greater scope to my love of discussion, and theoretical investigation.

Through Mr. Balch's invitation, it was arranged that I should spend my leisure time in his study, and prepare to preach the "great salvation." I know now, how little I was qualified and equipped for such an undertaking, but everything seemed possible to me then. The time I spent with him was serviceable in many ways, and by it, I attained some degree of culture, which otherwise might never have been enjoyed; but the teaching, and direction of thought, were too controversial, and disputatious to form the basis of a true culture. Mr. Balch was a man of much natural talent, but lacked careful training, and so jumped at conclusions, instead of proceeding through logical deduction. With great capacity for observation, he lacked the synthetic faculty for systematic thought. He stimulated one's desire to know more individual things, and to a greater love of mental freedom. He was a Democrat of the New Hampshire pattern, and although at heart an Abolitionist, his interest in the success of the party never flagged, until the control of the party was abandoned to the Hunkers, and fraternized with the "Silver Grey Whigs." Early in the War of the Rebellion he detected the centralizing tendency of the Republican party, and its evident fostering care of plutocratic trusts, and monied combinations. Although interested in him, to the very last, his course since the war, in relation to political partisanship has been little known to me. I judge however, he did not change his political or religious creed. He was gifted as an extemporaneous speaker, yet often confused his hearers, by rapid alternations of themes, and unconnected threads of discourse. He was on the whole of a just and generous temperament, but in which a natural acquisitiveness sometimes wrought a tumult. The memory of this kind, and almost fatherly interest in me, has by no means been dimmed by the half century of change, which has intervened; but it is sometimes relieved by amusing recollections of his parsimonious, and acquisitive peculiarities. He had assisted me pecuniarily in my time of study, and when I had obtained the ability to support myself, he asked me to give him a note, which I did. He kindly forbore to ask me for payment, but when, after two years or more I was able to pay it, I found he had calculated the interest, compounding it each year, and after the time I had removed to New York State, had computed it at seven per cent., the then legal rate there. I told him, the note had been made in Rhode Island, where the legal rate was six per cent.; that he had taught me "Gospel," and not "Law," and that the Bible condemned interest altogether. If he was right as to the law, he would have to go to law to collect his note. If he "appealed unto Caesar, unto Caesar he should go." Seeing I took the matter seriously he said he did not really intend to insist upon it. I refer to this, only as an illustration, that quite conflicting elements enter into the composition of the best of men.

When in 1847 the New York Association came down to Southold to narrow the Universalist platform, Mr. Balch sided with the reactionists, although he had ever been treated by them, as a sort of doctrinal Anarchist. He stopped with a Sea-Captain over night, who in talking over the situation said he had "never liked Mr. Ingalls, since he became so active in the Temperance movement, and showed sympathy with the Dorr Rebellion; but now, he puts the Bible under his feet. I'll be —— if I'll stand it, any longer." The humor of this, will be seen, when it is known that Mr. Balch had ever been conspicuous as a Temperance advocate, and had been compelled to leave Rhode Island, for his outspoken sympathy with Thomas W. Dorr.

In 1883, at about eighty years of age, he spoke to his old society in Bleecker St., New York City. I attended at the evening meeting. He was aged, and infirm, but the lineaments of the man of thirty-five were still plainly visible, and the volubility of utterance was still there. The sermon was on the Resurrection; Paul's fifteenth chapter of first Corinthians, being the basis. It took me back, nearly a half century, when I had listened admiringly to the same discourse—I say the same, although neither had been written. The manner, the treatment, and largely the language was the same. In religion, he had learned, and forgotten nothing it seemed, in that forty-five years since I had first listened to this same sermon.

After the meeting was dismissed, I sought an interview with him, and although it seemed difficult for him, to fully recognize his old pupil, he was cordial though expressing a regret at my agnosticism. How closely his character had held to its early tendencies, exhibited itself in the conversation which ensued with some of the monied men of the church, with whom he then and there made an appointment to meet in Wall Street, next morning, to invest in certain stocks, in which he was to give them, or be given points. Although afflicted with physical infirmities, most of his life, he lived to attain an age considerably past four score years.

CHAPTER V.

Of my studies in Theology and labors as a preacher, I have little to say; since they are hardly in a line with the social, industrial and economic investigations which have engrossed my more mature thoughts. I had spent a pleasant winter in Cape Cod in the beginning of 1840. Speaking at Hyannis, Yarmouthport, and Harwich, and afterwards visiting Southold, to which place I was called, and remained for three years. In 1841 I held a three days discussion, with Rev. Joseph Henson of the M. E. Church, and which reflected little credit on either of us, as it consisted mainly of quotations of opposing texts of Scripture, with more or less ingenious interpretations of obscure and conflicting passages. But, as I often think of it now, the Bible was vindicated from the charge of teaching unending punishment, in a future state of existence. It was in this year, that I was first able to get a public discussion of the usury question. Had often proposed it, in debating societies in Rhode Island, but only to be laughed at. Our society at Southold, entertained it only on condition, that it should be so worded, as to make me sustain the affirmative. In the discussion which followed, I had no assistance, but was allowed a number of opportunities to reply to the arguments on the other side. At that time, I had little knowledge of political economy, except what I had occasionally seen perverted in the political press; and Adam Smith, and his "Wealth of Nations," was wholly unknown to me, except in name. Nevertheless, I laid down as fundamental, that all wealth was the product of labor; that money nor capital of any kind had power of multiplying themselves, except by exploiting the fruits of labor; that labor produced wealth increased only arithmetically; while interest increased geometrically, and involved the absorption of all the wealth loaned, in every ten years; which was about the period of recurrence of our great finan- cial, and industrial crises. In the debate were two teachers from the Academy, two doctors, a lawyer, and a Judge of the County Court. They urged various platitudes, economic and ethical, but made no points, I was not promptly able to meet. They said that money, like commodities, was worth whatever it would bring, and they confound- ed use, with consumption. The principal of the Academy, desperate that no argument could stand against mine, finally endeavored to silence me, by saying that the earth produced spontaneously, and that it was just as right to take interest on money, as it was to take rent for land, or to sell trees growing on land that was bought for money. It was then, that I first saw the actual relation of rent to usury, and the injustice of the ownership of unused land, since it was able to exclude man from his natural environment, and labor from means of self-employment, and of certain subsistence. This, so excited the venerable judge, that he was only able to give utterance to exclamations, and opprobrious epithets, to the disgust of many who had come with the expectation of seeing interest completely vindicated. And the Professor only replied, that as he had shown that property increased through land ownership, he was under no obligation to defend that, and declined to say more. After the dis- cussion was over, a young man who had been about the world some- what, came to me, and said sympathetically, "You are right, I have seen, and noticed many things which confirm your views, and have no doubt that much of the general poverty of the world, and the re- curring failures in business, are due to interest taking." This was the first convert I had made, in ten years of talk upon the subject. Other warm friends, who could not account for the break down of the interest advocacy in the debate, still deemed me, a mono-maniac upon the question. After leaving Southold in 1843, one of my friends talking with another, who coincided, said, "Notwithstanding my great liking for Mr. Ingalls. I think his ideas about interest, are the silliest, I can conceive." I have had the pleasure of having both these friends, and many other friends of those days, admit that I was right, and that it was astonishing they could have been so blind. Another, some years later, told me, he had found no point in which his judgment in things, did not correspond with mine, except on the question of interest, that he could not see as I did, and all my arguments were without effect. He was quite prosperous then, and had both taken, and paid interest. At the breaking out of the war in "61," he met with business disasters, and finally went to St. Domingo, in search of gold. We had continued correspondence, and in 1865, I received a letter from him, expressive of disappointed hope, and broken health, in which he said: "Since I have been here, I have been thinking of our frequent talks of twenty years ago, on the Interest question. I could not see then, but I see now, that you were right. As I look back over the reverses of my life, I see clearly now, that ignorance of that question, has been the main cause of all my embarrassments, and but for which I should now be in easy circumstances, and my family in comfort." It was not long after this, that I learned, that his naturally robust constitution had given way, and that he had succumbed to the enervating climate, exposure, toil and mental care and anxiety. This friend was Captain Isaac Tuthill of New Suffolk, L. I.

After leaving Southold, I went to Danbury Ct., where I remained two years. I was then, recalled to Southold, and in addition to preaching assumed management of the Academy in 1845. But the confinement proved too much for me, and my health suffered. I remained however till the Spring of 1848. The action of the New York Association of Universalists, had divided our little society, into factions, more or less embittered with one another; and besides, I began to feel the pressure of the ecclesiastical spirit, and to desire freedom of thought, broader than their new made creed, contemplated.

Soon after returning to Southold in 1845, I had received from friends in New York City, copies of "Young America," a working man's paper, which drew my attention to the question of Private Land-Ownership, with great force, and at once convinced me, of what I had inferred, after the discussion on Interest, that usury of land, (rent) was the basic usury, on which that of money, and of other property chiefly rested. This paper was published by George H. Evans, an Englishman by birth, and a brother of the venerable Frederick W. Evans of the fraternity of the Shakers. He had previously published "The Man," and also the "Working Man's Ad-

vocate." "Young America", he devoted almost wholly to Land Re
form. He was assisted by John Windt, Lewis Masquerier, Allen E.
Bovay, Dr. Wilson, and a host of able correspondents, from every
State of the Union, among whom were Judge Waite of Illinois, Senator Walker of Wisconsin, Lewis Ryckman, and Gerrit Smith of New
York. In 1847, I attended the Industrial Congress in New York
City, and for the first time, became identified with the movement
for Land Reform. Here, I first met a number of men, of earnest and
devoted character, who never swerved from its advocacy while they
lived.

CHAPTER VI.

In 1848, I went as a delegate, to the Industrial Congress, which met
that year in Philadelphia. This, was the Presidential year, and
misled by the political spirit, the Congress resolved itself into a nom-
inating convention. I had here, my first inside view of political strat-
egy. Though of a mild form, it betrayed the peculiar methods of
office-seeking, which has from the first, disgraced our politics, and
has at last become almost unbearable.

The Land Reformers, wanted to make a clean ticket, with Judge
Waite for President, and Senator Walker, or Andrew Johnson for
Vice-President. But Mr. Evans, Mr. Windt, and Mr. Van Amringe,
were Anti-Slavery men, with several of the Pennsylvania, Western
and other delegates. After much electioneering, and some balloting,
Gerrit Smith, was nominated for President, and Wm. S. Waite, for
Vice-President. This did not suit some of the Land Reformers—especially those with party proclivities. John Campbell of Philadelphia, bolted outright, and went with the Democratic Party. One of
the delegates, boasted that he had come with the money of a prominent politician in his pocket. Notwithstanding this political epi-
sode, there was good work done, at this Congress. A number of
prominent men were present. Among them Mr. Van Amringe, A. J.
H. Duganne, John Sheddon, Lawyer Treadwell of Brooklyn, Theop-

hilus Fiske, J. E. Snodgrass, of Baltimore, Geo, Lippard, and many others, and when the merely political issues were not involved, the discussions were profitable, spirited and harmonious. In discussing the question of the disposal of the public lands, there was much enthusiasm displayed, and many euphemistic prophecies were indulged in, as to the progress that would follow the realization of free, and inalienable homes, under the contemplated Homestead Law. I remember Mr. Evan's speech, warning the Congress of the danger of indulging in too sanguine expectation of success, and urging unremitting action; launching out, into a semi-prophetic statement of what would be the consequence, if the purpose of the lobbyists, were carried out, to partition the public lands among corporations, and for the founding of immense estates, to reduce our people to the conditions of mere tenants, and dependent hirelings. He went on to say, that unless our measures were adopted soon, it would be too late, and the land once given up to the dominion of private monopoly, there would be no alternative, but the establishment of a landed aristocracy, and a titled nobility. Agreeing mainly with his forecast of the issue, I took occasion to say, that he did not seem to me, to have taken a sufficient extended view of the situation; that I had "enlisted for the War," and anticipated a life-long fight, and if after a life-time spent in the conflict, I could then see signs of a thorough awakening of the people, to the subject of labor's relation to the land, I could "depart in peace."

But the Congress adjourned and the delegates went home; some to work for the Ticket, some to work for the Abolition cause; but more for the Free Soilers, and a few for both the Democratic and Whig parties respectively. Judge Waite declined to run on the ticket with Gerrit Smith, and so there was no Industrial ticket in the field. We partially endorsed the Abolition ticket, and a few voted for it but I suspect that most of the Land Reformers, were seduced to vote for Van Buren and Adams, cajoled by the false cry of "Free Soil, Free Men." and other designing catch words.

Nearly fifty years has passed since then. A dozen years had scarcely elapsed, when in the very throes almost of national dissolution, a Homestead Law was passed; but so emasculated by political trickery that it has done little toward alleviating the condition of the increasing hordes of landless toilers. Advantage was taken of the good feeling effected by this act, to inaugurate a system of land jobbery, which has had no parallel in the history of land mal-appropriation. Many of the Rail-Road appropriations were already agreed to by the committee, ere the Homestead bill was acted on. Enough land was voted to railroads in a few years, to have given a farm of twenty-five acres (25) to every family in the Union. Subsidies of money, as well as of lands were voted to corporations, which have swallowed both lands and money, and swindled their stock holders as well as the people, by bonding the roads to themselves for more than the values expended in constructing and furnishing their lines. All that Mr. Evans prophesied has become true in the second generation, and labor has been reduced in this last decade of the Nineteenth Century to greater straits than under any system of slavery, or serfdom the world has ever known. But the necessity of recognizing man's relation to the land, and of labor to the opportunity, has meantime become widely felt, among workers, and every well-wisher of his race, as never before; and little doubt can be entertained that commercial feudalism, has nearly run its course, and must soon be supplanted by intelligent co-operation, and equitable division and exchange. It could not happen, but that the older barbarism of personal bondage must give way before the present more subtle form which controls the opportunity of the toiler, and all access to the passive factors of production, the field, the mine, the home, the shop and every sphere of activity, available to remunerative effort. If this does not also soon disappear, and become superceded by intelligent recognition of economic freedom, civilization itself, will succumb to the retroactive tendencies now in operation, and primitive savagery replace our moribund commercial monarchism.

It may be well to record here an incident that had occurred, a short time before the Industrial Congress held in 1848. The Land Reformers of New York City, had squelched the Whitney plan of building the Pacific Railroad, by pledging the public lands for that purpose. He had appointed a meeting of the Bankers and Capitalists, at the Broadway Tabernacle. He had made them a speech, and was preparing to organize a Company to carry out his scheme. He had not heard before, that there were Land Reformers; but he heard from them, that evening. As soon as he had closed his remarks, a call was made by them, (and they were there in force), for Lewis W. Ryckman, who took the platform, and made an eloquent, and most telling speech. After stating, in a careful manner, what must be the effect of betraying a trust, so vital to the well-being of the people, those who followed trades, as well as those who cultivated the soil, he demanded to be told, what the people had done, that their children who should dwell upon the fertile plains and the valleys of the West, who were to occupy, and improve them, should be doomed to lose their birth right in the Earth, and be made tenants and serfs, or helpless wage workers to the end of time, for the benefit of titled, or untitled lords, and soulless corporations. The effect of this speech, and the thunders of applause it awoke, fairly frightened Whitney, and his pals, and they left by the rear entrance, giving up the meeting to the control of the Reformers, who discussed, and passed pronounced resolutions against all schemes, for endowing Railroad Companies, or Syndicates with the inheritance of the people.

I had come to New York to reside, and was editing and publishing "The Landmark." Soon after the "Congress," I received an invitation from Gerrit Smith to visit Peterborough, and speak in Madison, Cayuga and Herkimer Counties. He offered to contribute twenty dollars towards my expenses. As it seemed probable that the circulation of my paper might be extended, I accepted the offer. Took the boat to Albany, and rail to Schenectday, and travelled by canal packet to a point nearest Peterborough. I enjoyed the hospitality of Mr. Smith and family, and attended a public meeting of the friends of the movement for Anti-Slavery, in the interest of their candidate, but as a Land Reformer, for they had a Land Reform plank in their platform.

I here met the Rev. Abijah Scofield, their preacher at Hamilton. He belonged to the orthodox wing of the free church movement, which was then making protests against the pro-slavery attitude of the Christian Church. He reported to Gerrit Smith, that he had to go away from home, the next day—Sunday—to attend the funeral of a deceased friend, and wished some one to supply his place in Hamilton. It was accordingly arranged that I should preach for him, the next day, although it was known to Mr. Smith and to Mr. Scofield that I was excluded from the New York Association of Universalists—that Infidel Sect. I preached in the morning on fraternity, and the necessity of charity and tolerance in the exercise of our religious duties, and in the evening upon land reform.

I spoke at Georgetown, Cazenovia, Oriskany Falls, Morristown, Hamilton, Madison, Pratt's Hollow, and other places, and finally attended the Free Church Convention, which gave a day to the consideration of the Land Question. I here met again, Mr. H. H. Van Amringe, who had come from New York to attend this meeting, with Mr. Evans, and Mr. Wm. V. Barr, an active Land Reformer of a vigorous intellect, and much natural facility of speech. I was both amused and instructed by a passage between Mr. Barr, and Mr. Beriah Green, whom he followed. The latter was President of a College at Whitesboro, and a strict constructionist of the moral and religious sentiment which pervaded a wing of the Anti-Slavery Crusaders. He met the demand for land, by a charge of irreligion, on the part of the laboring class, and of indifference to the plea for freedom for the slave. In following, Mr. Barr, apologizingly said, it might be presumption in him, to criticise his learned and logical friend. He had not graduated from any institution of learning, but from a shoe shop. "That is all in your favor." interrupted Mr. Green, "you did not have to unlearn so much you had been mistaught, as I had." Mr. Barr after sketching the situation of the worker, deprived of land and home, surrounded by the falses in business, and imposed upon by the educated fraternity of law, medicine and divinity, turned to Mr. Green, and demanded to know, how the ordinary toiler was to get proper notions of moral, and social duties. Mr. Green finally explained, that he in no wise desired to defend existing institutions, simply because they existed, but only so far as they could be demonstrated to be beneficent, but repeated his suggestion as to holding working men to the duty of siding with the Abolitionists, before they asked alleviation of their own wrongs. Mr. Barr enquired whether he would apply the same rule to the slaves, who not only did not protest against slavery, but were said to make the cruellest overseers, and when emancipated, and able, because the cruellest slave holders. And whether the laborer, ignorant and often as debased as the slave, should be held to the same degree of accountability, as those who had every advantage of circumstance, and education? Mr. Evans, Van Amringe, and myself were given also, opportunity to present our views upon the land question. Dr. J. H. Jackson, since of the Danville Sanitarium, spoke. Wm. Goodell, also. Many of the clergymen present, thought the land question was hardly within the scope of their purpose, although all were Abolitionists: many of them so radical, they—not only would not fellowship slave holders, but no church or membership, which did not disfellowship them. Gerrit Smith, also sustained our points in all respects, stating that the Bible was far more explicit in regard to ownership of land than in respect of slavery, and that if the holder of persons as property was to be excommunicated, much more should the holder of peoples' homes, and means of living. And moreover, that although the Abolition of Slavery, would not abolish land monopoly; the abolition of land monopoly would make slavery practically impossible.

Of this convention I sent this account to the Univercoelum:

Salisbury, N. Y., Oct. 10th, 1848.

Brothers Editors:

Having a few moments' leisure, I have thought to employ them in a brief correspondence. Some of the readers of the Univercoelum already know that I am absent from the city on a lecturing tour. Although the object was to advocate an important political Reform, I have nevertheless had opportunity to observe the spiritual tendencies in the region visited. Independence of all sectarian bias, has prepared me for the better consideration and arrangement of what elements, in the religious world, I have discovered in progress of change and development.

On the first Sabbath after my arrival in the interior of the State, I was invited to speak in Rev. Mr. Scofield's church at Hamilton. It was not inquired to what sect I belonged, for I was known to be a reformer; and the attention which was accorded me by these unsectarian people, who are nevertheless esteemed Orthodox, was flattering to one who has been marked as unsound, by a professed liberal and proscribed sect. The truth is, that there is a feeling among the noble hearted of all names, that this unbrotherly strife of sects is anything but christian: and that after all, he who has the spirit and does the work of a Christian, is most Christ-like. In this vicinity there are a number of free Churches, where reformers of all sects, and of no sect, assemble to worship, and hear the Gospel of Reform. Of course it does not essentially interest us to inquire, to what particular division they may have belonged, it is enough to know that they were zealously laboring in unison for the great cause of human advancement.

It was found not inconsistent with our object to be present at the Christian Convention at Canastota. Here were assembled some most earnest and advanced minds, to take into consideration the possibility of establishing a Christian union. The opinion seemed to prevail that in order to have union, it was necessary to have entire toleration. Resolutions were passed to this effect; also, that ministers might be ordained or chosen by the members, while any member had the right to administer the sacrament, or any other ordinance in which it is proper for an Elder to officiate.

It was gratifying to listen to the spirited debates which were excited by these and other resolutions. There were two or three who brought with them a portion of their love of Sect and forms; but they appeared like dwarfed minds, compared with those who unfettered, stood up manfully for liberty and truth. Here was Wm. Goodell, whose acquaintance would be interesting to any reformer. Linden King had come up from the depths of sectarism, to breathe an atmosphere of love and freedom; as well as his Son, who is early making the most rapid strides in spiritual advancement. Here was also the enthusiastic Pryne, whose whole soul seems to war with clerical assumption and domination. Here were other earnest men, from different parts of the State, and the blows which they dealt, against the hydraheaded monster, were neither powerless nor misdirected. The eloquence with which they plead the cause of oppressed and down-trodden humanity, bleeding under the severance of all brotherly ties, through mere sectarian prejudice, is seldom exceeded. For myself, there was much to rejoice at in the signs of progress here evinced, and in the manner with which every reference to the great ideas of the common brotherhood were received. Thus while

those preferring exclusive claim to these ideas, are treading the
backward road of forms and creeds, and sundering ties on earth they
believe will be reunited in heaven, true men are coming from the
precincts of every denomination, whose love of Christ is greater than
of a Church, whose devotion to humanity is greater than their rever-
ence for a creed. That their professions of liberality were not simply
formal, may be inferred from the fact that Mr. Van Amringe and
myself, were invited to take part in their deliberations, and that
what we had to say, was listened to with earnest attention.

That they are yet prepared for a general movement toward a
better organization, and a more spiritual union, may be questioned;
but the indifference of sectarian establishments to every form of oppression, and to all needful reforms; (especially, the subject of human bondage,) has opened the eyes of those who respect the rights
of man, to the enormous evils which have their origin and end in
this devotion to party and strife for denominational supremacy. I
ought to remark, also, that among the more advanced there are some
differences of opinion with regard to what constitutes a Church;
some regarding the church as a human, and others as a divine organization. Of the latter class, is Gerrit Smith, and there is a Church
at Peterboro' conducted in conformity to these views, and there are
several others in the state, somewhat different from what are called
free churches. In order that you may the better understand the
character of these bodies, I will give you a synopsis of the basis of
the Church at Peteroboro,' the form which I happen to have before
me. It is prefaced with a beautiful motto from D'Aubigne. "In the
beginning of the Gospel, whosoever had received the Spirit of Christ,
was esteemed a member of the Church."

You may be surprised to learn that after all, they have a Creed;
but it is, as Mr. Grosh would say, a very small one; nay, it is a very
large one; so comprehensive that all can be encircled in its embrace.
I will not give it entire; yet this is the Spirit of the whole. "We believe that the Church of Christ on earth, is composed of all the Christians on earth, and that the Church of any location is composed of
all the Christians in that location; and that members can neither be
voted into Christ's Church, nor out of it."

Such is the Catholic Spirit under which they meet; and it is unnecessary to say that freedom and comparative harmony are the result. Being released from the duty of inquisitors, they cheerfully perform the duties of members, and so far from squaring their opinions with an abstract formula, they feel free to express their peculiar views on all points. The following sentiments, in the form of resolutions, will further illustrate their conceptions of what a church ought to be.

"A Church of Christ is a company of moral reformers, and, any organization which refuses to engage in the prosecution of such reforms, especially those that are nearest at hand and most urgent, however excellent may be the character of individuals in it, is not a Church of Christ.

"Sectarism, guilty as it so clearly is, of rending the seamless garment of the Savior—of dividing the Church of Christ into mutually warring parties—tearing asunder those who should esteem themselves to "be One," even as the Father and Son are One—guilty also, as it manifestly is, of making the strongest and most successful appeals to the pride, bigotry and intolerance of the heart, is, therefore, the mightiest foe on earth to truth and reform, to God and Man."

"The members of a Gospel Church are not only free to entertain their respective views, both of doctrine and practice, but are bound to inculcate them."

An interesting feature of their "discipline" is to deal with scismatics, or in other words, those who circumscribe their christian sympathies within the limits of the Sects. If they find that any good man or woman has joined a sect or remains in it, they summon the person to answer to the charge of scism; and in several instances have succeeded in convincing them they had no right to give their affection to what they would admit was only a part of the true Church.

CHAPTER VII.

The New York friends, Dr. Jackson and several others returned with us to Peterboro from the Canastota Convention where we were tendered a reception at the residence of Gerrit Smith, and we held an interesting discussion on the reforms of the day, carried on mostly by Mr. Smith, Van Amringe, Barr, Evans and Dr. Jackson. For my part I sang Dugenne's "Acres and Hands," to an old English air "The Carrier Dove," to which I adapted it. Just before Gerrit Smith's death, some thirty years later, I received a letter from him, saying, he wanted to see Mr. Ingalls again, and hear him sing "Acres and Hands."

We had discussed the interest or usury questions, incidentally on that evening, Mr. Smith remarking that he saw nothing particularly wrong, in taking or paying interest; had himself done both, in the transaction of business, and thought he had been benefitted when he received it, and had benefitted others when he had paid it. A few years later, he wrote to me, requesting a formal statement of my views, on the subject, saying his wife said she could not reason the case with him; but she felt Mr. Ingalls was right. Whether my arguments produced any effect upon the minds of either, I am unable to say, as the Kansas Embroglio, fugitive slave law, and other matters of national concern, probobly absorbed the attention of such thorough Abolitionists.

Dr. Jackson, on the evening referred to, related an amusing incident, which turned a joke upon Mr. Smith. He had, after becoming a convert to Land Reform, made a speech at Syracuse, in which he had squarely taken the ground, that every man had a right to the land which he tilled, and that no one, had a just right to dispossess him. The doctor had met a countryman on the cars who said he had been to Peterboro, to see Gerrit Smith. "I told him," said he "that I had been unfortunate, that the season had been unfavorable, and the old woman sick, and that I could not pay the interest on the mortgage he held still on my farm." "I told him, I did not think he would trouble me and had told my wife, when she insisted on my seeing him, but that whatever came, I was going to rely on his Syracuse speech."

Gerrit Smith promptly on my arrival, had given me the twenty dollars, he had promised, and I obtained a number of subscribers for my paper, and besides had in some places where I had spoken, received some trifling compensation. Before leaving Peterboro, however, I sought an interview with Mr. Smith, and suggested that a little assistance would help me to keep the Landmark going, howevr disastrous the compaign might prove to the cause of Reform. He declined to assume any farther responsibility at that time. When however running for Governor in 1858, he placed with me five hundred dollars, to start a paper "The Land Reformer," advocating the doctrine, and his candidacy. But the time was unpropitious, and the means used for the purpose, was a dead loss. Seeing its failure certain, I suspended the paper, and returned to him, about half the sum.

When the Landmark was suspended in 1849, there was a foundation which would have served as a basis for a rallying point. "Young America" was declining—the Harbinger, and the Univercoelum were merged in the Spirit of the Age, edited by Wm. H. Channing, but which succumbed after a short life. Numerous papers through the the country dropped Reform advocacy, or confined themselves to the support of pure Anti-Slavery sentiment. Still there were friends enough to have sustained a well conducted reform paper, could it have been tided over the crisis. Whether Mr. Smith would assist or no was a matter for him to determine—I mention the matter merely as experiences I have met in reform work .

Mr. Smith's connection with the John Brown raid, has been a matter of grave discussion among his friends. Mr. Frothingham's, Life of Gerrit Smith, it is said, was suppressed, because it told too much truth. Brown visited Mr. Thaddeus Hyatt of New York, shortly before the raid, and told him, that Gerrit Smith had let him have money for the purpose he had in view. But refused to communicate his plan, because just then, Mr. Hyatt, pending the extension of his patent, could let him have none. Hyatt was summoned before the United States Senate, but refused to testify, even that he knew nothing of the raid, and defied it, though kept in jail for several months.

From Madison Co. I went to Little Falls, where I lectured and on Sunday spoke to a colored congregation upon land and freedom. At Manheim I tarried with Mr. Zenas Brockett, and addressed a meeting there, also at Salisbury where we met a brother of Mr. Brockett. After speaking, as usual I invited remarks, when the brother arose, and denounced me, and his brother also, saying we deserved to be in states prison, for advocating doctrines so destructive of the rights of property. Mr. Zenas Brockett was a pious member of the Baptist Church at that time, and taking opportunity he confidentially submitted to me his trouble as to what was duty with respect to it. I expressed astonishment that he should come to me, whom he must know, looked with little favor on ecclesiastical organizations of any kind. He thought, he said, I might give him an unbiassed opinion for that very reason. I asked him if his church allowed him freedom of expression, on the question of reform, in which he felt such deep interest. He said they did; but he did not know whether it was right to fellowship those who were indifferent to them. I said to him, that if in his place I should stay, and work where I was. If they could not tolerate me, I would go; but it was my opinion, that he should stay in the church and reform it, if possible, so long as he was in agreement with its religious teachings. Some ten years afterwards, these brothers came to our house in New York, staying all night with us. Mr. Zenas Brockett had outgrown his sectarian attachments, and the brother had cut loose from his party superstitions also. We had a most enjoyable visit.

At this point, I would like again to refer to Mr. A. Scofield, whose place I supplied at Hamilton. I enjoyed the neighborly friendship of Mr. Scofield, and his interesting family, some eighteen or twenty years later, both having moved to Glenora.

He preached hereabout, somewhat as a free lance, among the orthodox, and liberal Christians. He finally got into a discussion with Mr. Beach, the Professor of Greek in Starkey Seminary, the public meetings of which I attended. It was on the question of the "Godship of Christ." The one, contending that Christ was God and man—the other, that He was the Son of God. The discussion waxed warm, until parting on mere definitions, the discussion was declared off, on the second evening. For some reason or other Mr. Scofield wished that I should speak, as there was a considerable audience, and the evening was not spent. Rising, I said, it was to be regretted, that two such able men, were spending time and talent in debating questions, at best, purely speculative, while a world of misdirection ignorance and misery lay waiting the labors of the true disciples of the Christ of the Gospels. In referring to the discussion I said I had been impressed with Mr. Beach's profession of faith in the power of truth, and his statement, that only error feared investigation; but I did not think his charge of intolerance against Trinitarians, however it might apply once, in the times of Calvin and Servetus was true now, certainly not, as to friend Scofield, who twenty years before had invited me to preach to his people, and had now insisted upon my speaking to them, although fully aware of my heretical views. Simply as a test of his sincerity, I then offered to discuss with Mr. Beach the question of the pure manhood of Jesus, as set forth in the Gospels. He declined, giving as a reason, that the orthodox charged his persuasion, with teaching that Jesus was a mere man,—though many in the audience thought the opportunity should have been improved to clear up that very point. A lay brother was found however, to take up the challenge, but the discussion was not allowed to be held in the Christian Church. It came off in the little chapel, near Big Stream, in which Mr. Scofield was preaching, himself presiding at the debate.

I now resume, the thread of my narrative. Returning to New York, after my visit to Peterboro, and other places, I found the Land Reformers completely disorganized—the pruedo "Free Soil" party having by the usual duplicity of catch words and phrases succeeded in alluring many, by making it appear, that their pretentious professions of interest, had some purpose, or meaning. How sincere was their cry, maybe inferred when it is known, that the next election found the following of Van Buren, back in the Democratic Party, out bidding the primitive "Hunkers" in their subserviency to the dominant slave power, and outrivalling them, in their efforts to enforce the "fugitive slave law." It soon became evident, that Land Reform, and every progressive movement, must experience a set back from the reactionary tendency of things. I could keep the Landmark going, but it could no longer keep me going. I gave it up to a printer, William Haddock, who kept it running for several months. I constantly writing for it, without compensation, as long as he was able to publish it.

I received an invitation to speak to the Unitarians in Southington, Ct., and subsequently served as pastor there, for two years.

Early in November of this year, (1848), I was passing through Providence, and called on Mr. and Mrs. Dunbar B. Harris. I met there, and was introduced to George Bradburn, who quaintly said "I thought the editor of The Landmark was a bigger man." There was an anti-slavery convention in session and they insisted I should accompany them to it, which I did gladly. On entering Mechanics hall, we found the meeting just called to order. The chairman stated that the business committee, who had been appointed at the afternoon session, were still out, and that there was no regular business before the meeting, and called upon volunteers for addresses till the committee should come in. Mr. Bradburn immediately arose, and said that the editor of a Land Reform paper from New York was present and he, for one, was anxious to hear him speak upon this theme, and how it bore upon the anti-slavery question. The chairman promptly invited me to the platform. I took it, and thanked him for the unexpected opportunity, and supposing my time would be short, commenced without preliminary to explain the object of our movement—much to the following purport: Land is a necessity to life. The man, the animal, the plant, each die when denied access to the earth, and its growths. The right to life, involves the right to land to live and labor upon. Commercial ownership of land which enables one to exclude another from it, and thus enforces involuntary idleness, is as destructive of human freedom as ownership of the person, enforcing involuntary service. I remarked in passing, that our reform did not antagonize the anti-slavery movement, but complimented it—that Gerrit Smith, George H. Evans, John Windt, Mr. Van Amringe and many of our prominent men, were abolitionists in the strictest sense of the term. For myself, I had been a foe to slavery from my school days, when I read Cowper's touching appeal to England for its abolition. But that we had here a much more complex question than ever confronted England. Her slaves were thousands of miles away and could not compete with her wage workers at home. Ours were at home. Liberation of the slaves would bring

their labor in more direct competition with our over-crowded and
poorly paid wage-workers. I did not offer this as a reason against
the abolition of chattel slavery, but as a reason why the friends of
emancipation from chattel slavery, should unite with the friends
for the emancipation of the wage-worker, by restoring to him the
right to land, for the production of the means of life. I pointed out
that setting the man free, without allowing him access to the land,
would not benefit the slave, so far as the comforts of life were concerned, but would be a cruel mockery. That few instances of the
starvation of slaves could be found, while wage-workers and tenants
were starving by the hundreds, and the thousands, and sometimes
by the million, as in the then recent landlord famine in Ireland. No
menial, or even immoral service ever exacted from the slave, but
could be obtained by the landlord, or money lord, and at a price
less than the expense of the same service from the slave. No doubt,
but great cruelty is often perpetrated against the slave, but as a
rule he is better fed and clothed and sheltered than miners, or even
the agricultural laborers of England. No picture, general like that
of the miners of Great Britain, can be found in the slave-holding
states of this nation. There, men, women and children, bid adieu
to the light of heaven, from one week's end to the other, to dig the
black diamonds from the bowels of the earth; women are chained to
cars, and draw the loads, upon their hands and knees, where the
human form cannot stand erect. The agricultural laborers are not
as well housed and fed by the English nobility, and landholders, as
are their horses, or even their dogs. The real issue was between the
rights of man and the rights of property; between the rights of labor
and the rights of ownership. It was not the love of being a master,
but the ability to appropriate the results of labor, which made
slave-holding attractive. And it was not color or race-hatred which
lay at the bottom of the vulgar prejudice, and enmity of the white
laborer against the African slaves, so much as the fear that if liberty
was given to them, they would crowd him from his opportunity to
serve for wages.

I also remarked that the exigencies of the wage system, and of the
rent system, had more effectually succeeded in breaking up families,
taking away children and separating man and wife, than the chat-

tel system had ever shown, unless under exceptional circumstances.

After speaking for a half hour, I noticed the committee filing in, when, thanking the audience for their attention to the utterances of an outsider, I took my seat. Soon after commencing to speak I had observed the entrance of Frederick Douglass. He was then at the height of his popularity. Had just returned from his visit to England where he had been lionized, and patronized by the anti-slavery nobility, who had raised the money to purchase his freedom from his former master. He was not aware at whose instance I had been invited to speak. As soon as the report from the committee had been disposed of, Douglass took the platform, and began a reply to me. He said he had his idea as well as Mr. Ingalls, about the rights of property; but that the anti-slavery question was a totally different one. It was the question of liberty, not property. He had been in England and saw nothing of the pictures Mr. Ingalls had been showing them; and he depicted in roseate hues, the social conditions of English life. He deprecated the bare idea of comparing the condition of the English worker, with his freedom of person and surrounded by wife and children, with the chattel-slave, who was not the owner of himself, and whose wife and cshildren could be sold from him at any moment. In this vein he continued for a longer time than I had been speaking, then told the audience what they wanted. They wanted to have a speech from Mr. George Bradburn and some other speakers. They wanted to pass resolutions that had been offered by the committee, and to sing "Oh that will be Joyful," and they did not want to hear anything more from Mr. Ingalls. He had scarcely ceased speaking, when a vociferous call was made by the audience for Mr. Bradburn, most of the audience knowing that it was he who had introduced me. He immediately took the stand, and brought the people into genial good humor, by saying, with mock seriousness, "here Mr. Ingalls has been talking to you about wages-slavery, and Mr. Douglass about chattel-slavery—both have overlooked the great topic of the day"—he made an impressive pause, and then, "Old Zack is President of the United States for four years." This "brought down the house." Decisive news of the election of Taylor had been received that day. After referring in a satirical way to the great importance of the fact in our national history, he reverted again to us saying substantially "we need raise no question as to the veracity of either Mr. Ingalls or Mr. Douglass—the former did not speak of what he had seen, and the latter only testified of what he had not seen. He had been with those who were interested in having him see what was best not what was worst under English rule. Mr. Ingalls neglected to tell you, how he derived his knowledge—I will supply the omission. In substance it is from a report of the Parliamentary Committee, appointed to examine into the condition of the mining population and is quite as reliable, I think, as if it had been seen by either gentlemen." After the close of the meeting I was greeted by many friends, some of whom I had not seen for ten years, and also met a number of associationists who affiliated with the anti-slavery people. It was also arranged for me to speak in the same hall on Sunday evening—which I did, to a crowded house. It was the place of meeting for the Second Universalists Society, of which Rev. J. M. Cook was pastor, and to whose courtesy I was indebted for the opportunity.

Some twenty years later I read a report of an address made by Frederick Douglass at a colored people's convention at Lexington, Ky., in which occurred, words in substance, like these: "When the Republican party emancipated and enfranchised you, it failed in justice, in that it did not also award you land."

After the war I met Mr. Douglass at Waterloo, at a meeting of Progressive Friends, before whom I was permitted to present the Land and the usury questions and was treated with respect. I met at the same time Mrs. Lucy Stone, Mr. Powell and Professor Denton, all of whom listened with attention and expressed great interest. Mr. Douglass I met again on a railroad train, when an accident occurred which detained us several hours, and which gave us opportunity for comparison of views on many questions, on which much common ground of agreement was found. The last time I met him was on a Stonington steamer when going to Massachusetts. It was soon after the Freedman's bank swindle had been effected. I began at once to denounce that as one of the most dastardly financial outrages I had ever known, and expressed a hope that he could satisfactorily account for his relations to it at the time, as president. He begged me to believe that he was wholly unaware of the condition of the bank at the time he accepted the office, and that all knowledge of its operation was carefully kept from him till the crash came. He had afterward learned that his name had only been associated with the management of the bank to influence more victims to deposit money before the wreck was made.

Mr. Douglass has been eulogized as an early advocate of Woman's Suffrage movement and justly so. But in 1868, at the Equal Rights Convention in Steinway Hall, he claimed that it was then the "Negroe's hour,"—as the question of giving him the franchise was then before the country—and that woman should wait. In this he was opposed by Mrs. Stanton, Mrs. Stone, Miss Anthony and most of the advocates of equal rights, and among all the speakers at the convention was only supported by Charles C. Burleigh.

CHAPTER IX.

I first met Edward Kellogg, in 1848. He had just published his book on "Labor and Other Capital;" in later editions known as the "New Monetary System." It was at a public meeting of the Land Reformers of New York City. He addressed them upon the subject of Finance recommending government loans on real estate, at a low rate of interest. I felt it necessary to criticise the scheme, and stated that the result of his plan would be to give to large land holders the power to control the money of the country, to the exclusion of workers, and of business men. I had admired the sayings of Thos. H. Benton, "Old Bullion," as he was called, and the reformers, were mostly "hard money men," but they gave him respectful hearing. It first occurred to me, that a credit money might be serviceable, if it could be on a basis, not inviting to unsafe inflation, and the promotion of usury. It occurred to me also that the "legal tender" power of money was subversive of the principles of equity, and was essentially monarchical in its spirit, and tendency. I combatted Mr. Kellogg's idea that one of the proper functions of money, was "to earn an income for its owner." In an interview with him, after the meeting he expressed regret that he could not get the endorsement of the audience to his money system since his sympathies were with the toiling and dependent. Later I obtained his book, and wrote an extended notice of it, for the "Univercoelum," which appeared in two numbers, dated April 21st and April 28th, 1849 of that Magazine. In 1850 I called at his house in Brooklyn, and had a conversation of considerable length on the land and finance questions. He had read my criticisms, and admitted the points of danger I had urged; but having more faith in legislation, thought the rate (low) of interest might be determined by law, so as to keep down usury, and prevent increased monopoly of the land. In a subsequent edition, his daughter Mrs. Putnam states that he was, before his demise much exercised in his mind, as to what was a "true rate of interest," and that he had told her he had come to the conclusion that it was the "cost of issuing and maintaining the money in circulation." As the right to realize a gain from the use of money, anything more than the expense of making it, and keeping it good was a point we had especially discussed, it was gratifying to me to learn that he had abandoned entirely his theory put forth in the book that one power of money was to accumulate an income for its holder. His arguments against usury, and his illustrations of the workings of our existing monetary system, his generous sympathy with industrial progress and the well-being of the working people, made the book popular in the next generation, and a text book on finance for the movement in favor of fiat money known as the greenback party. Taking his idea of money leased on real estate security, and confounding it with government indebtedness, and his "safety fund bonds," with "the interchangeable government bonds," they proposed a mere fiat money, wholly incompatible with his scheme. His scheme would have been a sound financial policy and would have destroyed all individual opportunity for other banking; theirs would have secured immediate relief from the effects of contraction, but would have laid the foundation for the most reckless expansion, and ultimate public and private bankruptcy.

In 1848 I became acquainted with Theodore D. Weld, his wife Angeline, and her sister Sarah Grimke. While absorbed in the Anti-Slavery issue, they each had considerate thought for the wrongs of the industrious poor. I met at their house, Frances Green, John H.

Hunt ond Llewllyn Heskell. All were progressive people. Mr. Hunt was a brother of Freeman Hunt, the long time editor of The Merchants Magazine, and also of Washington Hunt once Governor of New York State. Both were friendly to our movement—John H. subseqeuently wrote the "Honest Man's Book." It was epigrammatic in style, and particularly lucid in statement, and treated the land and interest questions in a masterly manner. He was the first so far as I have been able to ascertain, who treated the land question in this country, as a political issue, which he did in a speech to the working men, in the New York City Hall Park, at the time of the "bread riots" in 1836. Mr. Freeman Hunt first called my attention to Mr. Kellogg, of whom he was an admirer, and to the money reform Mr. Kellogg advocated.

The "Honest Man's Book," was too true to its name, to be popular with business men. Too abstract to be attractive to the working men, even if they had greater regard for honesty than they display. But there was another feature which made it peculiarly inappropriate to the times—the breaking out of the rebellion. After completing his arraignment of the land and interest laws, in their work of plundering labor of its products, he attempted to forecast the terms of a truly natural government. And this, did not provide for the abolition of Slavery, directly, or other than as a result of social progress and of ecomonic law. This led his anti-Slevery friends to treat with less respect his principal subject and obtained him no friends among those who from principle, political bias, or business interests favored the "peculiar institution" of the South.

My stay at Southington has little that relates to the purpose of this memoir. I enjoyed perfect scope for theologic speculation, however heretical or sceptical. The leading mind in the Society, was Jesse Olney, a man of some reputation as a writer, particularly of school books. Several geographies and readers of his were very popular. He was a Democrat in politics, and less liberal in this sphere than in that or religion.

The movement in 1848 in Europe, had stirred deeply the sentiment of fraternity and justice of the American people: but the fiasco of the free soil party, and the success of the conservative spirit in the election of Taylor and Fillmore, brought on a re-action observed and felt everywhere. Failure of liberty in France, Germany and Hungary, discouraged the friends of freedom in all lands. 1849 was especially a retrograde year. My thought was all the while, upon the question of the land and the labor of the world, and though naturally fond of speculative discussion, the theological subtleties, and aimless syllogisms, with deductions from assumed or paradoxical premises palled upon my mind, and gave me a dislike for my employment. Several times, I had taken up questions with industrial bearings, but only to find, that if I spoke fearlessly, it irritated some, while those in whose interest I was really speaking showed not the least concern in the matter.

In this state of feeling I determined to resort to some industrial employment, and ultimately went to work at the bench, as a journeyman, in the fall of 1850 with J. H. Keyser & Co. corner of Cliff and Beekman Streets, New York City. Mr. Keyser was a friend of Geo. H. Evans, and advocated land reform at first, a graduated tax afterwards, to discourage the tendency to large accumulations; but finally came to regard the land question, as a "lost cause," as he himself termed it, after the immense subsidies of the people's land, were made to the railroads. He was a considerate, and comparatively just employer, and as such can only be remembered with respect. In the Tweed Ring affair, he was proved more of a victim, than an offender. But for twelve years, I had been engaged in study, speaking and writing on religious and social subjects, and associated with cultured and educated people. The change to a workshop at wages, with many uneducated and ignorant, vicious, and even brutal men was disheartening. Had I realized the full meaning to me, of my choice, I should have shrunk from the trial; but were it to do over again, I should make the same election. I had seen so many, who had embraced progressive views, and advocated them with great zeal; yet after having "run well for a season," become estranged, because the new advocacy could not give them a living, that for me. It was plain there was no other way, than to support myself by some regular occupation, and make my labor for the changing of human conditions, wholly a labor of love. Others entertain different views, yet follow them with equal devotion, but this course seemed necessary for me. From that time—more than forty-five years, I

have availed myself of every opportunity to speak on ethical and social subjects, without even getting travelling expenses paid, except
in a very few instances. Never have I received a dollar, for writing hundreds of articles for magazines or newspapers, drawing petitions, acting as Secretary to many movements, aid, and emigration
societies, and others. Have spent much money in publishing, or
getting printed numerous pamphlets, brochures, and one book of
three hundred and twenty pages. All with the understanding, that
everything received over and above cost, was to be employed in
extending such publications, and that nothing was to revert to me,
as profit, or as consideration for any personal service. It is needless
to say, that not one-half of the money so spent, has been made up to
me,—or is ever likely to be.

But I have no wish to communicate to others, the gloom of years
I passed through. Gradually the skies brightened, to be obscured
many times temporarily, till some twenty years passed away, since
which time I have been free from fear of poverty, and dependence.

CHAPTER X.

Immediately on coming to New York, I was associated again with
the Land Reformers. In the fall of 1850, I was called upon to preside at a large meeting at Tammany Hall, to listen to addresses by
United States Senator Walker of Wisconsin, and a German, whose
name I do not now recall, in favor of the proposition to make the
public lands, free to actual settlers and at one time it seemed quite
possible that St. Tammany would intercede with the "unterrified
democracy" to make that a party question. As the reactionary tide
of 1849 had reached its culmination, the workingmen began to move
again for some amelioration of their condition, in the shortening of
the hours of a day's work; by requiring that all public works be
carried on by government or corporations direct without contractor
or intermediate boss. A confederation of the trades unions was
formed, and periodical meetings were held in the old City
Hall. A few of the leaders of that movement were land reformers, but they were never able to enlist any considerable num-

ber of the union men to listen to the discussion of the land question. K. Arthur Bailey of the Printers Union, Benjamine Price, Andrew Day, Henry Beeny, Wm. Rowe, Robert Blissert, Leander Thomson, and Ira B. Davis were among those whose advocacy of freedom of public lands became outspoken and persistent.

When Kossuth came to this country he gave a reception to a delegation of working men and free land advocates, at the old Irving House parlors. Mr. Bailey was appointed to read the address, which was creditably written. After giving a brief review of the political situation, in this country, and in Europe, and expression of sympathy with Kossuth, and the lost cause in Hungary, the disposition of the public lands was referred to; the landless condition of our workers, and its effect in depressing the wages, and depriving working men of opportunities, and homes, were tersely set forth. In Kossuth's reply, he expressed his appreciation of the good will shown to Hungary's cause, by American working men, but reminded them, they had the franchise, and if anything was wrong in our administration, it was their fault, if they did not right it, at the polls. While thus administering a deserved rebuke to those working men, who were misled by party prejudice, and machine politics, he displayed ignorance of the fact that our evils have their origin in civil, and economic misrule, rather than in the political differences between the Republic, and the Empire or Monarchy.

After the experience of 1848, the Land Reform agitators had abandoned the idea of political organization, but they still kept up, an organization for purposes of propagandism. They questioned candidates for Congress, and quite generally voted for such as gave most favorable replies. They persistently petitioned the President and National Legislature. After the decease of Mr. Evans, and especially after that of Mr. Comerford, the labor of drafting petitions, and addresses fell upon me. From 1852 to the breaking out of the Civil War, no session of Congress, was allowed to pass without large numbers of petitions being pressed upon that body. These bore fruit, after the war had opened, in the passage of the Homestead Law. Benj. Price, Andrew Day, Henry Beeny, Wm. Rowe, and many others jealously gave their time to promote the agitation. The accompanying is a brief form of our petition.

To the Senate and House of Representatives of the United States:

The undersigned, citizens of the United States, feeling the urgent necessity of preventing the further absorption of the Public Lands of the United States by Railroads or other Corporations of having the Residue of said public domain forever set apart for the exclusive use of actual settlers, in limited quantities, Do Respectfully Petition your Honorable Body to take prompt action, to that end.

We urge our appeal on the ground that tens of thousands of the industrial classes of large cities and towns, now unemployed, must seek an outlet and escape from the poverty and distress which surrounds them, or rapidly be driven to pauperism and crime.

We urge our appeal on the ground of simple justice to our children and our children's children, and to the emigrants now seeking our shores, fleeing from the very monopoly of land so alarmingly threatening our Republic from the rapid absorption of the public domain by giant corporations and private monopolists.

We urge our appeal as a measure of justice to the whole American people. These lands are a rich legacy, held in trust by our generation for those who come after us—never to be alienated.

We urge our appeal finally, as one deeply affecting the morals and well being of our people, in that these giant corporations have become the allies of stock gamblers in turning our public domain (the heritage of all) into one vast gambling arena, in which though a few may be gainer and many must be losers.

To put a speedy termination to these threatened evils, and to secure a measure of equity and justice to the American people, we urgently pray the adoption of measures embodying the features herein set forth.

Leaving the employment of Mr. Keyser, in 1852, I engaged with Mr. Thaddeus Hyatt, and in 1853, while he was in Europe, managed his illuminated sidewalk business, then in its infancy. I found in him much sympathy for my social views, and our relations for several years were very pleasant. Business variances, afterwards, at times quite antagonistic, never—however on my part—resulted in unfriendly feeling—though some personal peculiarities rendered him greatly obnoxious to others who had dealings with him. He was generous and chivalrous in his advocacy of principle, and many a squattor in Kansas, and many a working man in New York has occasion to remember the generous Providence he proved to them. His labors and offerings in the free state movement for Kansas, is a matter of history, and also his effort to alleviate the distress, almost famine, they suffered in the winter of 1860 and 61. To illustrate his activity, he obtained from President James Buchanan, a subscription of one hundred dollars for the Kansas Aid Association, after the election of Abraham Lincoln to the Presidency and upon the eve of the Southern Rebellion. About one hundred thousand dollars was collected by the Association in New York of which Mr. Hyatt, John E. Williams, Daniel Lord, Messrs Seth B. Hunt, Mr. Elliot, Mr. McCurdy and others were the Executive Committee—Mr. Williams acting as Treasurer, and myself as Secretary. This money was mainly expended in shipping grain and provisions to Kansas, which were contributed in great abundance by Illinois, Indiana and the North Western States. Prior to this Mr. Hyatt had been through the ordeal of a contest with the United States Senate, on the right of that body to summon citizens to testify in regard to what laws were required to protect the country from occurrences like that at Harper's Ferry in the fall of 1859. He flatly denied the right, and was held as a prisoner of State. But when Congress adjourned, he was set at liberty, neither party wishing to take the responsibility of holding him, through the approaching campaign. The Atlanta Constitution gave the news in this form. "The fight between the United States Senate, and Thad Hyatt, has terminated—Thad whipped."

After the burial of John Brown, Mr. Hyatt conceived the idea of raising a fund for his family by disposing of a photograph of the old hero, of which he had obtained the negative of some photographer. By this means some $3,000 was obtained. When he was incarcerated the labor of this business fell to me. The Brown family were greatly relieved for a time by these contributions, and the reflection that this was being done was a satisfaction to him when in prison.

While Mr. Hyatt was in confinement some of the more radical papers had asked why the New York Tribune had said nothing on the subject. At length there appeared an article, half apologetic, and half condemnatory of Mr. Hyatt's course. I immediately addressed to him a letter, saying "The Tribune, has at last spoken, not in your defence, but in its own," and exposing its indecision, and lack of spirit. Mr. Hyatt enclosed this with a personal note to Mr. Greeley, requesting him to publish it, which he did.

While visiting Mr. Hyatt in jail, which I did many times, I often met there Senators Sumner and Wilson, besides several other Members of Congress, and was here, let into the ways of politicians. Judging from what I had seen in the Tribune, and other Republican papers, I conceived that the "border ruffians" of Missouri deserved only "shooting on sight," particularly two brothers, whom the Tribune thought, had names suggestive of what their fate should be—Stringfellows. General Pomeroy on the other hand had become particularly odious to the party, who were trying to make Kansas a slave state. One day while I was in conversation with Senator Sumner, and Mr. Hyatt, General Pomeroy was announced, and came in followed by a gentlemanly looking, tall westerner, whom he introduced as General or Colonel Stringfellow. Thinking there might arise a question of "coffee and pistols for two," I was somewhat startled. Presently General Pomeroy explained, that there was a land deal premediated, and that by uniting their forces, the leaders of the two warring factions thought they could secure the "appropriate legislation," they needed from Congress. They also wanted Mr. Hyatt to assist them with means necessary to facilitate the transaction.

General Pomeroy was afterward sent to the Senate, from Kansas, and came to bear the soubriquet of Subsidy Pomeroy, and of whom the anecdote is told, that on offering a certain bill, he felt called upon, to state, that there was no steal in it. Saulsbury of Delaware, immediately sprang to his feet and said "Mister President! I shall vote for that bill, for if anybody knows when there is a steal in a bill, it is the Senator from Kansas." Gen. Pomeroy was a man of kindly feeling, sincere anti-slavery man, a friend of Woman's emancipation, but without strength to withstand the corrupting politics of the time. When I remonstrated with Mr. Hyatt, for aiding Pomeroy with money in his political deals, he would say, "well!

the other party is using money, and he must, or get left, and the Border Ruffians will get into power."

After his release Mr. Hyatt had prepared, and placed in the hands of Mr. Gray the printer, a book containing an account of the proceedings before the Senate, in his case. And to which I wrote an introduction, taking up the Constitutional bearing of the question, and showing that inasmuch as the power to summon witnesses for the purpose specified in the summons, had mentioned only persons holding office, or employment under the government, it could not have been intended to embrace the ordinary citizen, and thus imperil his sovereignty. That the proceeding could not be regarded as a judicial investigation for no party was impleaded and in any case the Senate's judicial powers were confined by the Constitution to trials for impeachment. This book, although stereotyped, was never published, I think, as the breaking out of the Rebellion, and his appointment as Consul to La Rochelle, drew Mr. Hyatt's attention to more pressing questions.

CHAPTER XI.

A number of Reformers of the Individualistic school, were known to me in these years, but I had acted little with them, had read Dana's translation of Proudhon, had met Josial Warren, Stephen Pearl Andrews, and others of their school, and was impressed with the accuracy of their statement of the industrial, economic, financial, and social questions, but engrossed with the theory of Land Limitation, and which they seemed to ignore, I had not become closely associated with them.

The question as to the extent to which the principle of legal interference should apply in determining what is the law of economic and social science, had at the very first presented itself. I had avoided advocating voting and legislation, as too uncertain to be depended upon as long as error and passion swayed the minds of men. The state of economic and ethic relations had been relied on rather than appeals to political prejudices and material interests of the voters, immediate or remote; because a matter determined at the ballot box, or by a show of hands to-day, could be reversed to-morrow by the same process, while a principle once made clear would remain unaffected by popular caprice or misapprehension. The more I studied the question, and the history of legislation, the more it became apparent that what was needed, was a scientific solution, and not a political measure. Among the Associationists, as those who accepted Fourier's teachings, called themselves, with whom I was on terms of recognition were Albert Brishane, Charles Sears, John G. Drew, D. Munday, Benja Urner, with some slight acquaintance with Horace Greeley, Geo. Ripley, Parke Goodwin, etc. Between the Associationists and the Individualists, there was a wide distinction in theory, although a basis of common agreement in the estimate at which the conservatism of the governing class was held. All misgovernment and miseries of mankind were attributed by the one to our unscientific civilization, and by the other to the impertinent obstrusive interference of the dominating spirit of governments.

Confused by the claims of these differing advocates, who were agreed in this that society was all wrong, I sought a medium ground which recognized he right of the individual, without severing the ties which bind society together; which accepted the doctrine of equal freedom, as an hypothesis, by which to determine our degree of development from the past form and entanglements of social life. Seeing no escape from the despotism of the militant spirit pervading all forms of collectiveism, but though the attainment of exact knowledge, it appeared that no attempt at association was possible of success, except that which excluded the basic errors of vacant land ownership and the adsorption of wealth by the duplicate geometrical ratio.

Whenever approached by the Associationist or co-operationist to unite with them I demanded in any movement the free use of land, and freedom from the grasp of the usurer. This was deemed Greek or nonsense to the disciple of Fourier, with all his claim to science. And the individualist thought it a limitation to his personal liberty to be debarred the right to possess all the land he could buy, and to take or pay such interest as he and his customer cocould mutually agree upon. I am unable to say how many such movements I have been solicited to enter. Protective Unions, Co-operative colonies, Building, Land Associations, etc. I will only recite a few, and relate some facts coming under my knowledge of the workings of others.

The Brook Farm had existed and collapsed, before my interest was awakened in the social movement. Its early collapse was not due to lack of purpose or of ability on the part of its members, but to the neglect of economic considerations, and the impossibility of carrying forward so refined and aesthetic an endeavor, with so little amassed capital, in a community and under business relations, entirely worldly and predatory. What proved true in this effort at reforming social life, is noticeable in nearly every effort of the kind, which followed, however abortive. I refer to the fact that while every movement has failed, many individuals in each case have developed remarkable mental and executive abilities. The Brook Farmers evoluted into brilliant men of letters, journalists, and political Sages. Greeley, Godwin, Curtis, Ripley, Dana, have become historic names, and others equally worthy of mention have left their impress upon our times.

The most imposing of all attempts at Phalanx making was that at Ceresco, Wis. A large tract of fertile land had been secured, at the government price I think. For a while the pioneer work went bravely on and ultimate success seemed assured. But with success came the danger. The land in the vicinity appreciated. The "unearned increment," of the monopoly controlled acres was scented in the air, by the privileged cormorants, and a craze for land speculation, became contagious in the sacred precincts of the association, itself. The Phalanx collapsed because wealthy and prosperous in its more worldly sense. Warren Chase one of the original promoters, and at one time a member of the State Senate, was a conscientious land reformer, and would not engage in the scramble for the possession of land needed by others. I do not include him among the number of those who got wealth by the dissolution of the Wisconsin Phalanx.

The next if not the first in importance and longer sustained was the North American Phalanx, near Red Bank, N. J. Charles Sears was the business manager. The movement was inaugurated in 1843, and continued till 1859, twelve years or more. Mr. Sears joined M. Deboissier in an attempt to plant a colony in Kansas which though failing socially, succeeded as a business, in silk raising and manufacturing. I met Mr. Sears at reform meetings, and at mutual friends in New York, and several times visited the Phalanx. We often discussed the land and labor question, particularly as it was affected by interest and dividends to capital. I was invited to address the meeting of the members and visitors at one of their public gatherings, on which occasion the subject of capital in Association was critically discussed, and the impossibility of ultimate success, where the principle of paying interest or making dividends to capital was a permanent feature. So me remarks were made, by others, but no one attempted to controvert the positions taken. Much importance was given to the advantages of an associative life and industrial co-operation. Had I known that the question was seriously agitated the in Association management at the time, the utterance might have been more guarded, and I should have understood why the principle subject was not referred to by the other speakers. After the meeting was over, several persons before unacquainted, introduced themselves to me and expressed their concurrnce with my views among whom was Henry Edgar, a student of Comte and the positive philosophy.

The ostensible cause of its dissolution was the great fire, which destroyed their valuable milling property, and Mr. Sotheran in his "Horace Greeley and other pioneers of American Socialism," makes Mr. Greeley say that "there was no pecuniary failure in the ordinary acceptation of the term," since in the settlement "each stockholder received back about 65 per cent. of his investment with interest." But it is true that the struggle between those holding the stock and those who did the work, had reached that degree of intensity, that neither the persons representing the capital, nor the men who did the substantial work, were willing to renew it. A few individuals owned the greater part of the stock, and desired it boomed by declaring large dividends. On going down in the steamer, the year before the fire, I heard a conversation between one of the largest stockholders, and a friend in which it was urged that in order to make it a success, more liberal dividends should be made to induce larger investments. After Mr. Sears went to Kansas, in corresponding with me, he acknowledged that the dissolution though hastened by the fire could not long have been postponed, in any event, on account of the requirement of capital.

Mr. Sotheran, in his "Horace Greeley and other Pioneers of American Socialism," quotes Greeley as saying: "Blind competition tends to the formation of gigantic monopolies in every branch of labor; depriciates the wages of the laboring clesses; excites an endless warfare between human arms, and machinery and capltal—a war in which the weak succumb; renders the recurrence of failures, bankruptcies, and commercial crises, a sort of endemic disease, and reduces the middling and lower classes to a precarious and miserable existence." To all which a natural enquiry suggests itself: Has not the socialism advocated so strongly by Mr. Greeley—the Joint Stock method of business--been far more productive of monopolies, than any operation of the competitive system could possibly have become? Why not then remove the bandages from the eyes of blind competition, and allow the truth to be seen? Free and enlightened competition would have prevented and will yet destroy the gigantic monopolies, which the Joint Stock Association has fostered under Greeley's "idea of the sphere of Government." This, Mr. Sotheran has emphasized in his motto to the volume. "We believe that Government, like every other intelligent agency, is bound to do good to the extent of its ability—that it ought actively to promote and increase the general well being—that it should encourage and foster Industry, Science, Invention, Intellectual, Social and Physicial Progress." Now whatever may have been the ideal conception of Horace Greeley as to Social Life, it is quite evident from these quotations as well as from his practice in business and in politics, that his Socialism was of the state character, rather than that of the voluntary and mutual co-operation of individuals. His "Sphere of Government" embraced high protective tariffs, franchise to corporations, though he advocated general laws of incorporations, patent privileges, and the extreme interference of the governing power in everything deemed necessary "to promote and increase the general well being." In fact to Horace Greeley is due, more than to any other writer in this century, the overgrown corporations and syndicates, which he learned in the very last year of his life to comprehend, and to combat with which exceptional ability and chivalry, he finally sacrificed health, ambition and life itself. The dying eagle recognized as his own the quill which had guided the fatal shaft to his heart. Did the reflection that the mighty trusts and credit mobiliers, which crushed his hopes of political preferment, while throttling and paralyzing the industries of the land, had grown strong and powerful under the teachings of his facile pen?

Benja Urner had been identified with three Associative undertakings and witnessed their failures, ere he distinguished himself as a successful business man. The undertaking of John Wilkins and Gen. Guertner in Texas, The North American Phalanx, and the Raritan Bay Union at Eagleswood, N. J. This latter, as with all the others with whose history I have become thoroughly acquainted, split upon the same rock of the exactions of capital. Mr. Urner became an advocate of the Greenback heresy and later a convert to George's Single Tax doctrine. With Col. Daniels he established a weekly "Our Country" which had a brief existence. It advocated Fiat money, co-operation and nationalization of the land.

In 1850 I had through the Spirit of the Age, planned a scheme of an associative colony, which should be effected without depending on other capital than could be obtained by the working members themselves, by beginning in a small way and growing up from the foundation independent of tribute for the use of land or money. It was to form an organization of persons who were able to lay aside a small sum monthly. When a sufficient amount had accumulated to justify a purchase, select public lands were to be purchased, and a few earnest workers were to be sent forward to break up and prepare it for cultivation. Carpenters, masons, blacksmith and other artisans were to follow as fast as their labor should be in remunerative demand. And so build up a community where rent and interest and even speculative profit would be practically unknown, and the conveniences for social life, education, etc., be gradually and naturally developed.

I had extensive correspondence from many states. From Maine, Massachusetts, New York, New Jersey, Pennsylvania, Ohio, etc. But our organization was not perfected, when the Land Reformers of the city requested me to represent them in the Fourth Industrial Congress at Chicago, Ill. Thinking that the opportunity would be a good one to look out a location. I suggested to some of my correspondents, that I would have this in mind. From Chicago I came around the lakes to Cleveland, Ohio. And through Ohio to Pittsburg, where there were a dozen or more persons who had signified a disposition to be of our Colony. To my surprise on arriving, they had been led by a land agent to contract for a tract of worn out land on Bull Creek, in West Virginia, about equi-distance from Parkersburg and Marietta. At the solicitation of Oliver Peppard, I accompanied him to the place. Neither he nor myself were satisfied with the land or location; but some money had been paid on it, and so far as the Pittsburg people were concerned, their co-operation in any other movement was out of the question. On arriving in New York I received letters from a farmer in Maine, and two families from Massachusetts that they had sold out their places and were coming to join my colony. As no organization had been formed, no purchase of land made, and no payments of any kind received, this was a little surprising. However, when they arrived in New York I advised them to go to Pittsburg, where they found employment, and joined the "Valley Farm Association" in the Spring. Despite the unfavorable location, and the desultory way in which the movement was made, it was at first much enjoyed. Wm. E. Stevenson, who became Governor of West Virginia was an active member.

When the individual interest began to manifest itself, troubles about division arose, which required the exercise of much judgment and mutual forbearance. The result was that in a few years, all idea of co-operation disappeared, many left;—but for those who remained, comfortable homes and pleasant neighborhood remained. I visited them, or the families which were left, in 1860 and again in 1865.

With the utter failure to get any plan adopted or even understood, I abandoned the idea of becoming a Moses, or even a Joshua of an associate movement, but followed out the suggestion of making my reform work, a work purely of good will, and took up mechanical work as stated in Chapters 9 and 10.

Among the great number of Protective Union Stores, Industrial Co-operative movements, Land Purchasing Associations, etc., which I was solicited to join and from which I was debarred by their refusal to eliminate the charge of interest, it seems necessary to mention only a few.

A plan was formed to establish a co-operative colony in Louisiana by Thos. J. Durant, Col. Daniels of Virginia, and others. The plan had an attractive presentation, and I was earnestly entreated to lend my assistance and influence to it. I replied that I would, if they would leave out the interest the investors were to draw, offering to invest one thousand dollars, the principal of which only should hold as a lien upon the property of the Association. This was declined; then I proposed that the method of counting interest should be after the short method, ie. of calculating the amount on the whole principal, and deducting the endorsements with their accruing interests, until the sides were balanced, and the debt was cancelled. This would be doubling the return of his investment, to the capitalist in about thirty years, at six per cent., or in about fifteen years at ten per cent., which rate I should prefer.

This proposition being declined, I replied I could by no means be a party to a transaction which would bind labor to work forever, against a paltry investment of capital, embodied in plant which at least would require renewing every seven or eight years, but as a test whether their investment differed in any respect from its exploitive capitalistic brothers, I would propose that when the capital had been thrice returned in interest, the principal should be cancelled. To this no reply was received, and whether any progress was made with their speculation is unknown.

In 1879 I was requested to act as secretary to the Co-operative Colony Aid Association, to the formation of which, Mrs. Elizabeth Thompson was the main contributor; but who was seconded by a number of influential persons, among whom were Rev. R. Heber Newton and J. H. Rylance, Dr. Felix Adler, Mr. Jesse Seligman, Banker, Messrs. Montgomery and Saterlaa, Lawyers, and others. I served without compensation till the little colony was started. An organization of 50 or more colonists was formed of industrious persons, desirous to emigrate, and who held regular meetings in the office of the Association, 25 Cooper Union. A paper called "The Worker," was published and being asked to contribute I showed the dangerous nature of subjecting the colonists to a perpetual payment of interest at a high rate, or at any rate. This attracted the attention of some of the Association and when the matter of interest or dividend to the contributors to the fund was discussed, the manager was censured for allowing me to discuss the interest question in the columns of The Worker.

In October of that year during the visit of George J. Holyouke to this country, a well attended meeting was held in the large hall of Cooper Union, over which Rev. Robert Colyer was called to preside, Mr. Holyouke being the principal speaker. He dwelt more particularly upon the subject of co-operation in England, but showed how its principles might be applied to the successful planting of colonies, and the improvement of the condition of workingmen. Rev. R. Heber Newton then described the plan of the "Aid Association," and the work it had in hand. There was need, he said, of a movement "to enable the distressed laborer in great cities to go in goodly companies to places in the country, where they could live happily in co-operative villages and work together for each others good." The Rev. J. H. Rylance said he wanted merely to add "one cordial word of welcome to the gentleman who had addressed them","there was no truer apostle of human brotherhood than Mr. Holyoake, though he might discard the title of apostle. Colonization should have more attraction for workingmen and be of far greater importance to them than any political question could be. To help themselves was better than reliance upon Senates and Parliaments." E. V. Smalley claimed that the aim of the Colony Aid Association was an eminently practical one.

Dr. Felix Adler also made a brief address on the scope and import of the Association, and the prospects of its future attainments, which he thought would relieve overcrowded cities of their surplus population, while increasing the production of, and demand for labor.

When the rate was discussed I could have nothing to say, not being a member of the board, but only Secretary of the Association, but Mr. Seligman came to the rescue, unexpectantly to me. He objected to six or even five per cent., saying that the Association was organized to help, not to exploit the colonists; that six per cent. was impossible to be paid by more than a few of them, and so the land and such improvements as they should make would have to be given up after all their toil and privation. At his suggestion the rate was fixed at three per cent., which doubles in about twenty-five years, while at six per cent. it would double in twelve years, and in twenty-five years be quadrupled. that is be paid three times over without reducing the debt at all.

The organization of the colonists proved more effective than that of the Aid Association, since the means raised were sufficient to send out only a portion of their members, to say nothing of purchasing land. That was furnished in the last resort, by the donation of a section (640 acres) by Mrs. Thompson. The ability to collect funds had been greatly overated by the estimates of the finance committee. and the decease of one of the Seligman firm greatly discouraged their endeavors. As in other cases, I learn that to a portion, of the colonists. the movement has proved beneficial. but that all organization has been abandoned. and the struggle for existence there as elsewhere is proceeding on individual lines.

CHAPTER XII.

In 1872 our Association opened correspondence with the English Land Reformers. of different schools. as the following letters. first published in the New York World will show.

EXECUTIVE COMMITTEE LAND REFORM ASSOCIATION,

510 Pearl Street, New York City, June, 1872.

Gentlemen:—In a spirit of fraternal regard we herewith forward you a photograph of our Committee, mainly as it was originally formed thirty years ago. The devoted pioneer of our reform, George H. Evans, shown in the central figure of the group passed away fourteen years ago. * * * * We entertain towards you the sentiment which should actuate kindred workers in the same great cause. Our organization is formed for a single purpose—to abolish land monopoly—and we cheerfully co-operate with all who agree on this point. whatever be their views on finance or other political questions. Our great struggle for the last two or three years has been with the infamous land grants to railroad corporations on which have been squandered hundreds of millions of acres of the people's lands. We have aroused such a public sentiment as to extort from the minions of monopoly themselves the acknowledgment that they are satisfied the people will tolerate no further donations. The Homestead law, which we succeeded in getting adopted after a struggle of a quarter of a century, has been made available by hundreds of thousands of settlers who till their own soil in independence, notwithstanding that the law was so framed and has been so executed as to do monopoly the least possible injury. As regards the public domain we consider the contest about over. All parties now proclaim our policy, though politicians betray it whenever they dare. We are directing our efforts now to "Land Limitation," which term we prefer to "Nationalization of the Land;" for when no one can be protected by law in the ownership of more than a suitable maximum apportionment, no one can be denied its use. If the controlling title was in the nation a similar limitation would be required, for a monopoly of leases and special grants under Government for a term of years would work just as pernicious results as a monopoly of title-deeds or grants in perpetuity. We only need apply to ownership in land the old principle of law which forfeits a franchise by "mis-user" or "non-user," to secure all land not well cultivated to the free occupancy of those who would properly use and cultivate it. In your country, where independent holders who cultivate their own soil are the exception rather than the rule, as with us, different measures and methods of procedure may be required. But without presuming to decide what may be your best policy, we have stated the course which the reform we have equally at heart seems destined to take in this country. At the same time we greet with hearty sympathy the inauguration of such measures by you as you deem necessary under your condition to further this great and humanitary reform which seeks to make the earth as free to the willing toiler as the air he breathes.

Fraternally yours.

WILLIAM ROWE, President,

H. BEENEY. Recording Secretary,

J. K. INGALLS. Corresponding Secretary.

An answer was received from the Land Tenure Association, written by Mr. John Stuart Mill, his original draft accompanying the official document. The reply is as follows:

LAND TENURE REFORM ASSOCIATION,

9 Buckingham Street, Strand, W. C.,

October 10, 1872,

Sir:—I am instructed by the Executive Committee of the Land Tenure Reform Association to express their cordial thanks to the Land Reform Association of the United States for their friendly and sympathizing letter and for the photographs intended to preserve the memory of the founders of their body. Like you we had seen with regret and disapprobation the vast alienation of lands belonging to the people of the United States in gifts of private corporations, and we rejoice to learn from your letter that through the public sentiment aroused by your exertions this culpable squandering of the public property is not to be carried further. The aim of your Association is to compel the reservation of the remainder of the public domain for the exclusive use of actual settlers, but to these you propose that it should continue to be granted in absolute property, on the principle of the Homestead law, subject to forfeiture if not duly brought under cultivation. You, however, propose a limittaion of the extent of land which can be legally held in property by a single proprietor. Our own principles would have made us prefer in a young country like yours the State should avoid what we think the error of parting absolutely with the ownership of the soil. It is not for us, however, to attempt to impose our judgment upon you as to the particular mode of combating land monopoly which is most advisable and above all most likely to be successful in the United States. It is satisfactory to us to think that the grants of land to individuals need not be interpreted as waiving the right to take hereafter by taxation for the necessities of the State. a part of the increase of value which those lands will most rapidly acquire through the unexampled progress of wealth and population which distinguishes your country. This increase of value, as far as it does not result from the proprietor's own labor and outlay, but from the general prosperity produced by the labor and outlay of the entire community, we consider as rightfully belonging not to the individual but to the public, though we would carefully avoid exercising this right to an extent or in a manner which would impair the confidence of individuals in being allowed to enjoy whatever additional value may be given to their lands by their own exertions or expenditures. It is probable that this point may not have escaped the consideration of your Society, but that you do not consider the time to have come in the economic progress of the United States at which it can expediently be raised with a view to practical results. However this may be, and by whatever diversity of means our two Associations may aim at the same object, they are engaged in a common cause, and every step gained by either tends to promote the success of the other. For our own part we shall not fail to derive valuable encouragement from your example and sympathy.

I am, my dear sir, yours faithfully,

Thos. A. Cowper (Colonel), Hon. Secretary.

Mr. H. Beeney, Secretary Land Reform Association, U. S. A.

The other reply was as follows:

LAND AND LABOR LEAGUE, 80 WHITECROSS STREET, |

London, E. C., August, 1872.

To the Land Reform Association, New York:

Gentlemen:—We interchange with you the spirit of fraternal affection and feel our happiness much increased by communication with bretheren on the other side of the wide world, holding sentiments so much in harmony with our own and having one object with us, namely, the increase and lasting welfare of all mankind. The photograph of your committee so kindly sent to us will always be a pleasing memento that we are not isolated in our movement and will tend much to encourage us in our work. That for the Land Tenure Reform Association has been duly transmitted, and its acknowledgement will doubtless be accompanied with copies of publications issued by them, in which you will observe that they make honorable mention of our League and really admit the truth of our principle while they waive the advocacy of right and substitute that of expediency, in many instances by argument more in harmony with our position than their own. Although there have been

among us, in times gone by, men who maintained the principle we
now publicaly advocate (as your quotation from our own Black-
stone shows,) yet it is but recently that such a Society has been
formed; and we believe that we may claim the privilege as ours.
You will also be glad to hear that the platform of our League has
so far progressed that no advanced liberal organization is now
called into existence which does not indorse our chief proposition,
"The Nationalization of the Land," while other associations follow
us to a great extent. Accept our hearty congratulations on the
result of the great struggles you have brought to such successful
issues as to prevent any further land grants and to have established
the Homestead law. Glorious results! repaying all your long ener-
gies many thousand fold in the gratitude, freedom, honor, and independence of the hundreds of thousands of settlers from many nations
blessed through your instrumentality with a true, natural, and lasting patrimony. Comparing the two countries, your vast, and, as far
as human wants are involved, boundless continent, and our small
islands of the United Kingdom, a different policy is necessarily required; for while you, with your unlimited acreage, may say to land
monopolizers, "Thus far but no farther," we see all our land monopolized, either totally or partially, and all our people—as well as
our million of paupers—divorced from the soil and that natural
right to appropriate sufficient of it for their beneficial use, entirely
ignored by royalty, aristocracy, the Government, Church, and plut-
ocracy. The principle we maintain is that land, in justice to mankind in successive generations, cannot rightly be private property,
and hence private ownership of land is condemned by us and neither
grants nor leases in perpetuity are countenanced, but simple tenure
under the State, and that, too, contemporaneously with its proper
cultivation and use, and forfeiture by misuser or non-user. We
may enlarge the quotation heading your letter, and heartily say,
"The land shall neither be sold nor granted forever;" and in so doing
we feel we do not violate that sacred law, but only extend its power
to crush the monopoly of inhuman and avaricious men. We look
forward to the time when social and scientific advancement shall
have so far progressed that every nation shall be highly productive in its manufactures and agriculture; that in proportion as ap-

plied science supersedes labor in the world, the now doomed life-long toilers among us and other peoples shall be relieved from over-wrought work, and shall be enabled to enjoy, without anxiety, a life of comfort, happiness, mental and moral elevation, in a state of society based upon the nationalization of the land, as the natural, inalienable, and everlasting right of man throughout all ages— that right to the land conferred upon him, in truth and equity, by our all-benevolent Creator. Earnestly wishing your Association long life and prosperity in its work, we subscribe ourselves, in behalf of the Land and Labor League, your brothers in the cause of humanity.

JOHN WESTON, President, etc, etc.

In giving the above correspondence to the public, we deem it proper to add a word in explanation of our views in regard to private property in land, and which we hold rests, precisely, as all other private property, upon the ground that "it is the product of one's labor." It is economically as well as morally wrong to bar access to the raw material, which needs the application of effort to convert it into wealth. Opportunity has justly no price; but, as referring to the land, should be shared by all according to the capacity and desire to cultivate and improve it. During the employment of one's labor, and the reaping of the fruit, the right to private property, in the soil, is as sacred as in any other thing; for, since labor can effect matter by moving it, and in no other way, the soil, which one's labor has moved (in the direction of production) is as veritably his own, as the gold he has dug from the mountain, the fish he has taken from the sea, or the game he has captured in the forest.

We are unable to foresee any danger, from the civil acknowledgment of this right, to the principle of "eminent domain," or "right to tax," in the State; but on the contrary, judge them more secure as well as less liable to abuse, when the soil is under the control of its honest cultivator, than it could possibly be under any system of allotment by lease from the Government, which method could hardly fail to induce corruption; by the opportunities it would afford for favoritism.

The enormous increase in the price of land near our business centres, on close investigation, we believe, will be found to arise from the unjust power to hold lands in unlimited quantities, and from the ability of the classes, living by the privileges it confers, and the speculative trade it fosters, to pay immense sums for the monopoly it creates, and not through any normal progress in wealth and population. This increase is an appreciation in the trade price merely, and not in any value or ability in the land, to yield a more bountiful return to labor, or greater facilities to industry or social intercourse: and represents neither private nor public outlay or labor, but only the power to bar the industrious poor from the passive elements of production.

All price, other than that which represents so much labor performed, but unrequited, and which it is urged should be reclaimed by society, we recognize as the result of pure monopoly; and which we should aim to destroy rather than sanction, by making the State a partner in the imposition.

With one-half of the agricultural laborers of this country, proprietors of the acres they till, we think the time not yet come for the adoption of any plan to tax away these increased values. And we trust in our ability to make it appear so clear that this increase is due wholly to the unlimited power given by our present laws of acquirement with privilege to monopolize the soil, as to compel the adoption of an effective limitation, which shall remove the necessity of its consideration for all time.

We have already a precedent in our State Legislation, where the issue on this question has to be met, limiting the amount of realty which religious and other corporations may acquire; and the only thing really necessary to be done, is to apply the same principle to acquisition by the individual.

By order of the Committee.

J. K. INGALLS, Cor. Sec.

CHAPTER XII.

The discussion of the land question, had gone on in this country for forty years or more, mainly on the issue of "Freedom of the public lands, and later on the Land Limitation, when a new and disturbing element was sprung upon the movement by Henry George's "Progress and Poverty." The English Land Reformers had for many years advocated the "Nationalization of the Land." The English system of land tenure was derived from the feudal system, making the crown, the ultimate source of title. No absolute or Allodial title was known to English law. The orderly way to secure equal opportunity for the occupation and use of land, would seem under these conditions to have the nation resume ownership, and rent the land on equitable terms to the citizen. Such a plan might or might not be connected with the collection of dues or taxes for the support of the government, since there are many ways in which governments could be maintained, without directly taxing the products of labor applied to the land.

George's remedy can hardly be classed therefore with Land Reform, since it is at best, a Tax Reform. How it could be made to work with the allodial title which gives to the grantee, and "his heirs and assigns forever," absolute title to an estate, is not readily seen. I grant property may be confiscated; but it must be where treason or crime of an aggravated nature has first released the government from its obligation to protect the citizen. For our country this form of taxation is not reform of any, kind but revolution.

Before Mr. George entered his teens, Patrick Edward Dove, had perfected his scheme in his "Theory of Human Progression" and buttressed it with all the logic and lines of argument, and illustration adopted thirty years later by Mr. George. This I pointed out in the columns of a New York Journal a year before Mr. Sullivan in Twentieth Century, labored to show that George's scheme, was a plagiarism from Dove. I made no such charge, but certainly the similarity of the plan and the mode of argument would seem convincing in the absence of Mr. George's positive assertion that he had never read Dove's book, before publishing Progress and Poverty. Mr. George had been familiar with the Evan's school of Reformers and long before his larger book appeared, had pointed out that limitation to private ownership of land would prevent land monopoly.

Soon after the appearance of Mr. George's book I became acquainted with the editor of the Irish World. In reply to some of my strictures on George's scheme, answers were made over the signature of Gracchus, which were thought to be from Mr. George. Here follows a contribution to the Irish World, only a part of which was published. In a speech he had made in Dublin, Mr. George said: "To solve the land question and the money question it is merely necessary to take for the benefit of the whole people, those fruits coming from the land, which are not due to the exertions of labor or use of capital of those who are engaged in using it." Nothing is said here about nationalizing the land.

Doubtless, Mr. George would be unable to find even in Ireland an instance where, the landlord being a judge, anything more than these fruits were taken as rent. The only difference between this plan, which Mr. George was careful to state was not "Mr. Davitt's particularly," and current landlordism is that in one instance those fruits go to a class, and in the other to the whole people; in other words, to the ruling political party or administration. He does not stop to consider that this circumstance would in no sense change the immoral nature of the tax, however it might mitigate its public impolicy. As to the portion of fruits which are to go to the use of capital employed in cultivating the land, it would be hopeless to find any farmer or operator in any field of industry to admit that more was now received than was their due. Political economists do not admit any such thing, and we look through "Progress and Poverty" in vain to find any such intimation from Mr. George.

That Mr. George aims at the same general result as other land reformers, I have no doubt; but his premises as to the use of capital and its reproductive power, together with his theory of rent—that it is the result of something produced by the land without labor,—is wholly unsupported by any known facts; and his plan of taxing back what is wrongfully wrung from labor under this false pretense can but prove delusive. If successful as a tax, it would to that extent prove useless as a measure of equity. If successful, as he con-

ceives, in giving every one a foothold on the earth, it would cease
to yield any revenue whatever, and thus prove self-destructive, for
no one not deprived of land by law or force would pay rent to government or landlord.

The farther discussion of the question was put in the form of

DIALOGUE.

Jonathan—Good morning. George. I am glad you have called. I
am becoming deeply interested in the land question. To me it
seems of importance to other countries as well as to Ireland, and
that we cannot fully sympathize with the movement there until we
understand it as a problem of world-wide application.

George—You cannot be interested in a question of deeper importance, and you are right in thinking it a subject of universal concern. The monopoly of the land in every country lies at the
foundation of class domination and of the poverty and industrial
subjection which prevail widely even in this land of civil and pliti-
cal freedom. Private property in land, whether under inheritance
or commercial traffic, necessarily ends, sooner or later, in its absorption into the hands of a small and privileged class, while the majority of the cultivators, and, indeed, all workers, will be reduced
to the condition of tenants, wage-workers, and tramps.

J.—That is also my thought, although I am not certain it could
not be so defined and guarded as to make it operate in favor of
equal opportunity and equal security. For instance, here I own forty
acres. This would interfere with no one's opportunity if some were
not allowed to buy up hundreds and thousands of acres, not for the
purpose of cultivating or occupying, but to hold them against the
poor and homeless, in order that they may tax the toil applied
in their cultivation and prevent those who need from going upon
them and making homes.

G.—I see you have not studied this land question in all its phases.
Private property means property, and, if you attempt to guard or
control it, it ceases to be such. I think nationalization of the land
the only practical solution of the question, and that can be most
readily effected by taxing back the value of the land—i. e., the rent
which it will bring—for the benefit of the whole people.

J. The nationalization of the land in a comprehensive sense is a thing generally admitted, I think. No one disputes that the land of any country belongs to the whole people of that country. The only question is, how can the principle be applied to protect the individual in his natural right of access to his normal environment so as not to invalidate the right of "eminent domain," which is exercised more or less widely and wisely by the governments of all countries, and which by the genius of our laws is supposed to reside in the whole people? The whole people cannot be evicted. It is only by allowing the individual to be evicted and debarred from his natural inheritance that society can be endangered by land monopoly. Society has, therefore, an undoubted right to prohibit the occupancy by any person of such extent of the common inheritance as would crowd or exclude the weakest member from his foothold on the soil.

To levy taxes for the accumulation of an indefinite sum, for which expenditures have to be found, is to create a fund inviting corruption and speculation and the betrayal of public trusts. No experience which any people in any time have had would justify it, and it could not logically be sanctioned by anyone but the advocates of the nationalizing of industry as well as of the land, and of wholesale governmental co-operation, which would make the government the employer of all labor and the determiner of all wages. I do not understand you to advocate this.

G.—However I may agree in the abstract with what you say. I cannot avoid seeing that it is private property in land which is the foundation of the evil. Abolish this by making the nation the owner, and, of course, no such thing as monopoly could exist. You must admit that to equally distribute the land among the people would be impossible, even if desirable, which it is not. Many want no land, but all are entitled to their share of what it produces, minus the amount justly due the cultivator, and minus the part rightfully due the capitalist, who has furnished or advanced means to furnish the stock and general plant employed in cultivating the land.

J.—And the cost of collecting and disbursing the same among the whole body of claimants?

G.—Yes; but that is unavoidable, and must be considered as compensated by relief from all other forms of taxation. I was going to add that rent is an economical fruit not the result of labor, but in addition to it, which the holder of land who cultivates it himself receives over and above the compensation of his labor as truly as the idle landlord.

J.—Is rent at the same time, then, "an immoral tax," as Mr. Davitt asserts?

G.—Yes, when paid to landlords, but if paid to the government, and by that applied to the public welfare, each member of the community gets his just share of the natural produce of the land. Rent, economical rent at least, arises wholly from the different fertility of special soils, as explained by Ricardo and other political economists.

J.—I am not unaware of that, or of the use Malthus and other writers have made of this theory to satisfy the laborer that eviction and starvation are in the order of Providence and not the results of unjust and barbarous laws of tenure. That under any system of freedom of the land there would be a choice of locations and of qualities of the soil there can be no doubt; that parties would be willing to pay something for such choice there can be as little; but that such transactions would degenerate into fixed rents, without landlords, is hardly conceivable,—not certainly while as at present there is abundance of land of good quality to produce all that is necessary for the public consumption. The inhuman mockery of this plausible theory is all too apparent when we reflect that much of the best land even in Ireland is now untilled, while tenants are being evicted from the poorest because they will not pay a rent at a rate almost, if not quite, as high as the best land would command.

G.—It seems to me you treat the rent theory with too little consideration. It is very clear to me that rent only represents the difference between the productiveness of the best lands and that which is not sufficiently productive to yield rent. If the cultivator owns the land himself, this production in excess of that of poorer land which is cultivated is a gratuity to him which comes from Nature, and not from his toil, since he has toiled no harder than the man who has produced the smaller yield; and the only way to equalize the award of industry is to tax away this excess and give it to the public. The theory is in itself so plain and generally accepted that I wonder you have the courage to dispute it. Mr. Mill denominates it the "pons asinorum."

J.—I know it, but was always in a doubt as to his application of the term. It might be that he meant such a bridge that all asses coming near would be sure to go over. It is not so much the theory as the use which is made of it that I deprecate. That there is difference in soils and in the desirableness of situations is true enough, but that such difference constitutes the entire rental is too absurd for serious discussion. For, then, if all soils were equally fertile, and all situations equally desirable, no rent could be obtained, however the land might be monopolized. The inequality which would arise from the working of lands of unequal fertility is greatly overestimated, and could be remedied by much easier and more natural methods. With a rational system of limited occupancy the restriction would embrace the consideration of superior fertility, and with more land of an inferior quality, with more varied crops and careful tillage, all serious inequalities would be overcome. The man with easier tillage and more productive soil will be able, doubtless, to obtain the same price for his grain or fruits as the man with poorer soil and shorter crops. He will have somewhat more to exchange, and will with the excess purchase luxuries. This, while it may stimulate other industries, will not increase the cost of any necessaries to the neighbor. The rent theory goes always upon the notion that the best land will keep producing bountifully year after year and generation after generation. This is folly. Land, however fertile when first taken up or when it first comes into the possession of the cultivator, will soon work down to a condition where it will do no more than is done for it. The original difference of most cultivable land will soon disappear under an equitable system of apportionment and intelligent use.

G.—Well, I came to read you a lecture on this subject, but you have read me one. I have never heard the "rent theory" attacked in this way before. If rent means only the different degrees of productiveness of different soils, there seems force in your suggestion that then no rent could be collected if all lands were equally desirable. But it is quite apparent that landlordism could not stand on any such position as that. I shall have to modify the statement by saying that under private ownership of the soil monopoly is enabled to exact the difference between the production of the best land and of such land as would be worked for its entire product without rent.

J.—Adam Smith asserts wages to be the entire labor product. Ricardo, the author of the "Theory of Rent," consistent with his theory, makes bare subsistence the natural rate. If this is true, as it must be, or the theory of economic rent be abandoned, then rent begins at this end and not at the excess end of the industrial problem, and does not absolutely require that any but the poorest lands be cultivated to produce a rent, if such lands will yield anything besides a bare subsistence to the cultivator.

Whether this theory would work if left to the operation of natural laws is another question, which it will be time enough to examine when our laws are repealed and equal opportunities are enjoyed.

It would be very easy to show that commodities have a price only because there is a difference in their quality, etc. For instance, the price of potatoes is only the difference between the size and quality of those most desired and those which are so small and of so poor a quality that they can be had for nothing. But an economist who should attempt to incorporate such a circumstance into a basic economic prinicple, and seek to tax back the whole value thus found for the public use, would simply stultify himself.

Your mistake arises in supposing that there is such a thing as wealth produced without labor. With equal access to the earth and its natural and spontaneous productions, the labor of gathering is all there is of production, and all that one man can justly exchange with another is the service he has rendered in such gathering. And that, in the absence of monopoly, is all that can have price. How one who stands aloof and does nothing towards this gathering can claim a portion of the wages of the gatherer is not consistent with any conceivable system of equity. Only upon repaying the service rendered is he entitled to any interest in the thing harvested, and then he receives under an equitable exchange the same proportion according to his service as the man who gathered.

In this way the right of soil is essentially vindicated. The artisan, artist, teacher, litterateur, and follower of any trade or profession is protected, for each requires and usually consumes quite as much of the earth's products as the cultivator, and that, too, without rendering disproportionate service. Why, then, should the cultivator be taxed to benefit the others? Under free land or effective limitation of its ownership it would be optional with anyone of another calling who felt he was unfairly treated to plant and gather the fruits of the earth himself. All this would require no complicated scheme of taxation, no cumbersome official machinery, but simply a repeal of the class laws of tenure and the extension of the principle of limitation found so salutary in all other matters of civil rule.

G.—In view of all you have said, I still think that rent arises, to an extent, at least, from a gratuity of Nature," and does belong properly to the whole people, and I see no better method than to tax away this gratuity from the landlord for the benefit of all.

J.—Without arguing that point farther, it really appears to me that to estimate that as a gratuity which is acknowledged to be "the price of monopoly," is illogical in the last degree. If nature has gratuities, it is for those who gather them. With equal opportunity if any refuse or neglect to gather them (not infants or disabled), they have no equitable or moral claim upon that which others have gathered; for, by rendering a reciprocal service in that which they prefer to do, they can secure what they need. Whether any such thing as economic rent exists at all can only be determined in the absence of monopoly. That rents are greatly above any possible bid for choice, and wholly separate therefrom, is seen by the fact that, where highest, premiums are often paid on leaseholds. Taxation on a basis so indefinite, so wholly dependent on monopoly and the limit of endurance which the poor will sustain, is as devoid of economic judgment as of democratic simplicity.

G.—But an end must be put to the oppression of landlordism, and, as the land cannot be divided in such a way that all shall share its benefits, I know of no other way to make the thing equitable. The tendency of productive industry to consolidate itself in the hands of large corporations must necessarily extend to the cultivation of the land, where it is seen that a few large enterprises can be carried on much more successfully than many small ones. To divide up the land into small holdings would be detrimental to production, as is held by many writers.

J.—But many writers of eminence take an opposite view, citing France, Belgium, Switzerland, &c. But, though the issue is at least evenly contested, I do not propose to make a point of that. Even if wholly as you say, in its mere relation to production, it would not be conclusive. There are other and broader questions than that of large production. The maintenance of the fertility of the soil and the development and improvement of the individuals of the race are aims to which miner economies should be sacrificed, if need be.

G.—You will admit that the "division of labor" has exerted a powerful influence in that direction!

J.—Certainly; but you must also admit that, carried to the extremes which are exhibited in our large manufacturing establishments, it tends to reduce the worker to a mere appendage of a machine, and can have only one effect,—the deterioration of all manliness and the destruction of all self-respect. The pointing of a pin, as a continual employment for twelve or fourteen hours a day, can end only by reducing the man to an automaton. Large production of pins can well be sacrificed to a greater diversity of employment for the individual, and the development of a higher manhood; if not in the interest of simple political economy, at least in the higher interest of social economy.

G.—My plan embraces the idea of "giving to every man that which he fairly earns," and to capital what is "due for its use;" but that which goes as rent to the land I would have divided equally among all, since it belongs to all. Interest on money and profits derived from commodities in process of exchange and distribution are different in their nature from rent, and are realized "after labor has been duly rewarded."

J.—I am sure that economists seek to draw this distinction; but it is wholly chimerical. The union of capital with labor is no more complete than that of the land with labor. No essential difference can be shown between rent, interest, and profits.

Rent is the interest upon the money for which the hired land would exchange. Interest is the rent of the land which the money would purchase. It can make no possible difference to the farmer whether the sum he pays is paid as rent or as interest on the purchase money of his farm. Both the rent and interest may be loaded with expenses, taxes, repairs, &c., but stripped of all these, they are identical in this: they are a tax upon the production of those who work for the benefit of those who do no work. Profits are also loaded with costs of superintendence, expenses, &c. Stripped of "dues for service," however, they are identical with rent and interest,—an "immoral tax" on the productions of industry.

G.- But you forget that I assume that rent arises not from the labor, but independent of it, as taught by all political economists. And it is to tax that back for the benefit of all that I am contending. The question of interest and profits is held to be different from rent; but your way of putting it is novel. Yet it seems to me these are both right, and would work no great evil but for a monopoly of the land.

J.—But these, in common with rent, take so much from the annual production of labor, without any return whatsoever, when stripped of the extraneous portions with which they are usually connected. I think I have satisfactorily shown that rent arises in no such way as claimed, but wholly as "a monopoly price;" that wealth has no such power of increase as is claimed in justification of interest or usury; that trade has no power to multiply wealth, and that commerce can only add to the wealth of society by performing specific service in its production where and when needed for consumption, and that, when such service is fairly rewarded, nothing remains for profits but an immoral tax.

G.—But surely you do not propose to control interest and profits as well as rent? That would involve a degree of governmental supervision which I am sure would be repugnant to the spirit of any free people.

J.—Doubtless; but the dilemma is yours, not mine. I was just going to say that, waving my objections to the "rent theory," admitting the power of wealth to increase of itself without labor, and of commodities in process of exchange to multiply on the hands of the holders,—though each proposition is vastly absurd,—the conclusion is unavoidable that interest on money and profits on trade are equally gratuities arising in Nature, to which all are equally entitled as well as to the economic rent arising from the land. How you can logically refuse to tax back the money and trade values, if any such naturally exist, as well as the land values is a matter of great wonder to me.

G.—But I see no other method of redressing the great wrong of land monopoly, and, that evil obviated, it seems to me that the other evils would remedy themselves, if they are evils.

J.—That is also my belief. In your plan, however, I see no certainty of remedying the basic evil. To do away with land monopoly only one course is open,—abolish it, as chattel slavery was abolished. Repeal all laws giving titles to land and make occupation the only valid tenure. This would do away with all discussion as to the nature of property in it.

G.—But the difficulty still remains. Equal distribution is impossible. Besides, some want much land, others little, and still others none at all. "Nationalization might be changed to Townshipization,"* and so the local government, whatever its form, have control. The large holders would then share, under the system of taxation, with those who held little or none. Each would rent of all, and so the values be equally distributed.

J.—I am very glad to hear you say this. It is one step more in the right direction. This would approach nearly to the ownership in the township or village community, once the general system of land tenure in Europe. A step or two more will place you on solid ground. The familization and individualization of the land follows as a logical sequence from your admission.

G.—But you do not notice my point that many individuals do not want land at all.

J.—I was about to say that it is untrue. Every individual needs a place to live and work in. Thus far the wants of all are nearly equal. We are "tenants in common," upon the bosom of mother Earth, and no one has any just claim against another for obtaining that which with equal opportunity he declines to appropriate. His refusal to occupy proves that he estimates his advantage greater not to occupy, and that all assumed advantage to the occupier is quite if not more than compensated through reciprocal exchange.

There exists no reason why any one should hire a home which does not apply with greater force to the reasons why he should own it. Even a single room can be owned, since it can be hired. Requiring to change his residence, one would experience no more difficulty in finding a purchaser than would the landlord (nation or township) in finding a tenant for it. Any disposition of the land which does not embrace the private ownership of home and the normal environment of the individual will not be the final one. Under that, even the changeful and migratory would find no serious inconvenience, while the many would enjoy, in its security and stability, a permanent reliance, and, in its healthful stimulus, the noblest incentives to beautify and adorn the limited portion falling to their control.

---

*See Henry George in "Irish World" for August 26, 1883.

CHAPTER XIII.

The testimony delivered before Mr. Hewitt's Labor Committee in 1878 was in part as follows:

Hon. A. S. Hewitt, Chairman Congressional Labor Committee:

Dear Sir:—On the day I was invited before your Committee, I was unable to remain until my name was called. I have, therefore, prepared a paper, and would be glad to have it submitted to the Committee. I also enclose a "Memorial of the National Land Reform Association," which has already been mailed to the Members of both Houses of Congress. That contains sufficient suggestions upon our Public Land Policy, and also some useful hints as to Finance.

Respectfully, etc.,

J. K. INGALLS,

Corresponding Secretary National Land Reform Association.

The real causes which produce periodical depression of business and destitution of the producing classes are to be sought in the imperfect knowledge of the general principles of civil and economic law, and in the chronic misgovernment resulting therefrom, rather than in any of those superficial circumstances, or matters of legislation, which have chanced to accompany or immediately precede those revulsions.

It is illogical, for instance, to refer them to the cost of our civil war, or the destruction of property by it; for nothing is more familiar to the student of history than the rapidity with which nations often recover from the devastations and losses of war, when the spirit of the people is not broken by oppressive and unequal laws. Instance the recuperative power exhibited by France in her recovery from her late war with Germany, and her indemnity of a Millard to her successful foe. In our case, the loss must have been mainly replaced within eight years after its close, or else it is difficult to understand how there could exist an over-production, which throws labor out of employment. That it is not a disproportionate production, as claimed by Prof. Sumner, before your Committee, is proved by the fact, that the depression is not confined to a class of interests or industries, but prevades all, with unimportant exceptions. Could the Professor's astute thought have been directed to the manifest disporportionate distribution which occurs from causes I shall attempt to point out, it would not have been so fruitless.

Theories of Protection or Free Trade may be applied in explanation of the suffering in special lines of business or of industry, but that they can effect such general consequences, is simply absurd, and even if such unreasonable results could be logically ascribed to them, we should still be no nearer a solution of our problem, because the nations representing the extremes of these respective theories are equally as great sufferers as ourselves.

That the increased employment of machinery has had the result of displacing labor to a considerable extent is doubtless true; but it is also true that the construction of such machinery and its requirements of constant superintendence and repair, has absorbed much of that displaced labor, while it has greatly cheapened and extended the consumption of the manufactures it has apparently over-produced.

Its present use is not so much to be deplored on account of the numbers it displaces from special employments, as for the unequal distribution of the results of its production, and which awards to labor not a moiety of what it produces, while to capital, in the form of profit, interest and rent, it surrenders the remainder, and thus enables great numbers to live upon the product without labor or service to society of any kind whatever.

We have, then, no recourse, but to look into our system of civil and economical legislation, to solve our problem. We are told, with great deliberation and show of knowledge, that "nothing can be done by legislation to relieve the present distress," and if we are compelled, logically, or otherwise, to accept this conclusion, as regards labor and the condition of the poor, may we not be allowed to enquire into the workings of that legislation which has been so lavishly bestowed, particularly during the last fifteen years, upon speculative schemes, to aid moneyed corporations and enterprising adventurers of every description; and to give fortunes to those who live by profits and interest drawn from the products of industry?

From the first our legislation, State and National, has been under the influence of a Lobby, constantly increasing in its unscrupulous and relentless grasp of power, and which has often become thoroughly organized for the promotion of schemes of aggrandizement wholly incompatible with the public good.

And must the unfortunate toiler now be told that legislation, which has done so much to hasten and intensify this catastrophe, cannot be expected to do anything to relieve it? Surely workingmen, unschooled in the subtleties of our current "Political Economy," may be pardoned for having dreamed that a government. which had freely voted such subsidies of land and money to private corporations; such franchises, as actually abdicated its own right of "Eminent Domain," might devise some practicable relief to the idle hands and starving mouths of those who had produced the wealth thus handed over to organized rapacity.

I am fully aware of the dangers and difficulties which attend legislative interference in questions of this nature. Had our remonstrances for more than a quarter of a century been heeded, the immense domain, now held by railroad corporations, or organizations growing out of land grants, would have been in the hands of hardy pioneers, whose identity of interests with the best good of the nation, and the independence which self-employment begets, would have been a perfect safeguard and barrier against the extreme agitation in business or in politics which now threatens the stability of our institutions. Abundant supply of food would have been secured; a steady increasing market for our products of the shop and factory, and a healthful, because stable, growth of all our industries.

Society, by its civil laws and positive enactments in regard to real estate, has sanctioned and reinforced this assumption or usurpation of the elder and stronger brother, instead of protecting the interest of the minor and weaker. But the time has now come, especially in this republican land, which has embraced the theory of making all "equal before the law," to take the administration out of the hand of him who has so grossly violated his trust, and re-apportion this patrimony in the interest of all.

The result of this assumption of private control over unlimited extent of the soil, is first, to enable the owner to exclude from its occupancy or cultivation, all other persons, who will not pay him tribute in money or in kind. This removes him entirely from the operation of the law of competition in the exchange of services, while the wages laborer, as Mr. Thornton has shown, is alone subjected to a forced and unnatural competition. Land monopoly places a "monopoly price" upon everything produced or gathered from the land. I am aware this point is denied by writers who have followed Ricardo, but I am also aware of the specious, not to say superficial reasonings, which they employ to evade a point Dr. Smith made irrefutable.

Accumulations of wealth (or stock) under the operation of this arbitrary control of the soil and the ability to purchase into this class monopoly, has given to money its unwarranted power to obtain an income for mere time use. Now, while the accumulations thus withdrawn from the productions of labor are constantly returned to business, by being reinvested in productive industry and healthful enterprise, the hurtful consequences which follow are not apparent, but, as the process of accumulation and absorption goes on, extravagance and speculation gradually develope themselves, until they assume absolute control of all industry as well as trade. Confidence is then weakened. Capital is withdrawn from investment. Prices fall, and a general shrinkage of values of all the products of labor, and, necessarily of wages, takes place.

The terms of these crises are sometimes considerably extended, and their results intensified, by the employment of an expanded circulating medium and of business credits. This reacts upon the real estate market, running up lands in favored locations to fabulous prices, and so, when the extreme has been reached, there being no farther recourse, the crash comes. With the day of payment, property has to be sacrificed to meet obligations, shrinkages take place, which fall wholly on that portion of the capital employed which is not subject to the liens of secured debt. The ruin of the debtor is completed, and to the loss of all creditors who are unsecured. The means of employing labor are lost to those who would employ it, and the laborer is thrown out of work. Now, this crisis, which brings such disaster to business and suffering to labor, becomes the harvest time of all such capitalists as have managed to keep their credits well secured; properties often falling into the hands of the parties who sold them, at one-half the price originally paid.

Dr. Smith describes such capitalist as a "person who has a capital from which he wishes to derive a revenue without taking the trouble to employ it himself." ["Wealth of Nations," c. 4, closing paragraph.] In other words, one who wishes to obtain the services of others without rendering any service himself in return. By the time these crises occur, this purpose has become a mania—to derive an income from labor without even giving it employment.

It will be found that these crises have occurred since the formation of our government (and Mr. Horace White says, for the last two hundred and fifty years), at quite regular intervals of about ten years, which neither protective legislation, free trade acts, change of the financial systems, nor even very destructive foreign or civil wars have been able greatly to vary. Now, this period is about the same as that in which a debt at seven per cent. per annum, compound interest, becomes doubled. That is to say, that if the whole capital of the nation is loaned at seven per cent., and the interest compounded, in a little more than ten years the entire capital of the country will be required to pay its own interest. Hence, repudiation of the principal becomes inevitable, or else the endless perpetuity of the debt, absorbing the complete wealth of society in every decade. Fortunately for mankind, the former obtains to a large extent, and thus periodically, though extensive bankruptcies and suspensions, the clogs are removed from the wheels of industry and of business, and they are allowed to move on again, till the return of another period.

Mr. White is evidently misled by his references to the failures of the last five years. The whole number of bankruptcies may show not much over five per cent. He does not say that it shows only five per cent. of the capital previously employed which has been wiped out during that time. An estimate of the general loss to the country through failures, suspensions of Banking, Insurance and Railroad Companies, and various speculative enterprises, would probably treble that rate, and, taken in connection with the reduction of the capitals through shrinkage of values of corporations, firms and individuals still remaining solvent, with foreclosures on properties, which have not been sold for enough to meet the mortgages, and all those sums previously paid on property which has been lost on foreclosures, fifty per cent. would be a much nearer estimate to the amounts cancelled without consideration than five per cent. Statistics on all these items would be difficult to obtain, but that losses in the various forms in which they have occurred constitute a large proportion of the capital employed in 1873, does not admit of question.

To show with greater distinctness, the operation of the principle which produces these crises, let us suppose that, instead of the large proportion of the capital of the country, which is let out at interest, the land should be so loaned, and further suppose that, instead of the annual percentage being paid in money, it was stipulated to be paid in kind. That, as interest on money is paid in money, so the rent or interest on land should be paid in land. A man borrowing land on such conditions, would, in a dozen years or so, pay back as interest all he had borrowed, and must of necessity, repudiate the principal—become bankrupt in land. For it is evident that in the period in which the payments of interest would amount to a sum equal to the principal, an amount of land equal to itself, would be required to be returned to the owner for its own use, and as the amount of land in any town, state, nation, or the world, is a fixed and definite one, the operation of any such stipulation, as a rule, would be impossible, and besides producing untold embarass- ment and suffering, must end at last in repudiation. A system of contracts like the above, would be held in any court as invalid, because they involved conditions well known to be impossible.

But the operation of our credit system, and payment of interest on capital to those who take no care in its employment, virtually involves the same consequences. With the accumulations of interest upon a given sum, the possessor can purchase a given amount of land in every period, corresponding to the amount of the principal invested. This enables the capitalistic class, as distinguished from the industrial or commercial class, to control the ownership of the land just as effectually as the titled nobility of any country ever did. Already in our older states, the number of landholders are rapidly decreasing, although the genaral population, particularly in cities, is largely on the increase, thus continually augmenting the dependent or wages class, and rendering any emancipation there- from more and more hopeless.

Access to cheap lands has, on each recurrence of a crisis, hereto- fore opened an avenue to our surplus labor when thrown out of employment and also extended the market for our manufactures, thus operating both ways, greatly to relieve the depression. But all our great railway facilities have not kept pace with the rapacity of the land-monopolies, and a settler now, to obtain public land, must take himself twenty or thirty miles from any thoroughfare, and wholly out of social and congenial life.

All our boasted improvement in facilities for travel have not helped the dependent laborer. His natural powers will carry him as far as his days' wages will transport him on our subsidized rail- roads.

Government may wisely repeal all such laws as facilitate the alienation of the public lands. It may refuse to sanction contracts pledging the homestead for debt, or to enforce the collection of any debt, the amount of the principal of which has been once paid in interest. It may provide for the rapid payment of the public debt, or its change from an interest-bearing to a non-interest-bearing one.

In fact, the war debt has already been repaid. Much of it has been twice paid, and some of it has been three and four times paid, in the form of interest and premiums. To legislate so that this species of property may be maintained at par, after being three times paid, while all other property has depreciated one-half, or more, is to villianously discriminate between classes of people who hold different kinds of property, and in favor of those who render no service to society. That the public faith should be held sacred; that the validity of contracts should be scrupulously respected; none will deny. But public faith is due to the humblest as well as to the proudest of its citizens, and as fully to a doer of a day's work as to a holder of a government bond. If either cannot be paid without ruin to the other, the situation is one that demands compromise and composition.

The taking or paying of interest has been condemned by every moralist, from Aristotle and Moses to John Ruskin, of our own time. In every seven years, Moses, the great Jewish lawgiver, provided for the cancellation of all debts, and at the fiftieth year by the re-apportionment of the land. In our times of rapid accummulation, debts on interest should be held cancelled at least after ten years payment of interest. It is seen now on economic principles, that the system of usance is as destructive to our material prosperity, as it has ever been regarded detrimental to morals and the discharge of human duty. Government then, should discourage, not sanction it, and clearly define the kind and nature of the contracts it will attempt to enforce.

The superstition of the trader or money-lender should no more form a basis for legislation than that of a religious devotee, who wants God put in the Constitution, that his views of what he conceived to be His will may be enforced upon the people.

Much could be done by refusing to enforce claims for the payment of interest, except where payment of the principal was withheld for the purpose of injuring the party to whom the debt was owing, or for arrears of wages not exceeding one month. Granting credit and incurring debt are in no wise economic acts or necessary transactions. They give no increase to social wealth, nor any healthful stimulus to productive industry. The government may rightfully refuse to rectify the mistakes which people make as to whom they will trust, or the value of the securities they may take.

It is a matter of public notoriety, that our Patent Laws are no longer serviceable as a means of encouraging useful invention; but are mainly availed of to foster monopoly, and promote rapacious schemes, through combinations, which use them to terrorize those employed in legitimate business through fears of vexation and costly litigation. Those laws should either be wholly repealed, or so modified as to render monopoly of the manufacture, or of trade in patented articles impossible. This might be done by allowing the inventor to collect from those who made or sold a limited fee for a limited time; without interfering in any way with the regular course of competition in any business. As now interpreted, our Patent Laws are a source of immense evil, injurious to commerce and every sphere of industry, and constitute a nuisance, which should be abolished.

In 1883 I was before the Senatorial Committee on Education and Labor and submitted the following:

I am requested by the Executive Committee of the National Land Reform Association, to submit to your consideration the following statements and suggestions.

1. The sustenance of human life and the satisfaction of material human wants, are wholly supplied by human labor, from the land and its resources.

2.—All social wealth is the product of labor, intelligently directed: but without land and the opportunities which occupancy of the land affords, man's exertions can produce nothing or even be put forth.

Hence the right of life upon the earth for any and every human being depends upon his right to occupy the land, and to improve its opportunity to labor. It also follows that whoever lives without labor of his own, lives from off the labor of others.

From the earliest times productive labor has been burdened and despoiled. Ownership of the laborer, in barbaric days, was the method by which the dominant class appropriated to itself the greater share of all industrial productions. With the disappearance of that servitude, however, the appropriation of the products of labor, by those who do no labor has not ceased. The man who owns the land, eventually owns those who live and labor upon it, and is able to appropriate as large a share of the production as if he owned their persons. From our laws of private ownership of land, unlimited as at present, grows the privilege to exclude all persons, and to prohibit the application of labor, except upon such terms as shall please the owner.

The founders of our government supposed they had remedied the evils attending the British Landlord system, when they prohibited titles of nobility, and abolished the ancient right of primogeniture and of entail; but the potency of all these adhere to the system of private property in land, which we have retained, but which ignores the restraints or responsibilities which characterize the Feudal system.

There are numerous estates of great magnitude in our country which are growing larger each year, and which date back to the last century. More than one of these in this city has steadily advanced for three quarters of a century, and is now in possession of the fourth generation, and is virtually entailed by the possessor deeding in his lifetime the property, mainly to his eldest or favorite son.

The friction of this system of industry and trade falls mainly upon the relation between wage worker and employer. The presure under which both at times suffer and which induces the antagonism between them, lies deeper than the inequality of compensation. Unless the employer is also capitalist and landholder, or in combination with these, as in the large corporations, he cannot, however disposed, greatly wrong labor, and cannot seriously oppress it at all, but that it is homeless and landless, on account of a monopoly of the only opportunity of employment, the land. This alone causes the constant increase of the class of wage workers, for which there is no corresponding increase of demand.

I have thus briefly sketched the forces which operate to produce the poverty and distress of the disinherited toilers upon our common inheritance. That personal indolence and improvidence contribute to the destitution and suffering which exist I do not deny; but they are often if not mainly induced by the system of wages itself, which divorces the worker from any personal interest in that which he produces, and also by the spectacle which our society presents, where honest labor is despised, and luxury is the reward, not of toil, but of idleness and vice, and also by the success of the cunning and unprincipled, who succeed without either honesty or labor, in acquiring wealth and position.

I deem it useless to devise schemes to remedy these evils. Only a return to natural law, and a scientific adjustment of the two primal agents in production, land and labor, and the restoration of man to his normal environment, can effect any salutary change.

Our national domain is already well-night given over to monopoly. Enough to form seven States like NewYork has been bestowed upon corporations, and the right of eminent domain nearly abdicated by our Congress.

I hold this tendency even more dangerous to our national well-being than the wild speculation in lands which seized the wealthy men of our country at the close of the last century, and until the passage of the Homestead Act. These efforts were intended as speculations, and were liable to tumble, as they did. This however, is a maturer purpose to establish large estates and a general system of rentals, or of bonanza farming, which makes the cultivator of the soil necessarily a tenant or wage worker. So far has the system operated to depress the condition of labor, that our corporation magnates, and even your committee deem it worthy of remark, if found that labor is better paid in this country than in the tax-ridden and ill-governed countries of Europe..

The only legislation that we would suggest is the repeal of all land laws, so as to leave no protection to land titles not based on personal occupancy, and give no one power to take back two values where only one has been received, or to tax labor for privilege to work with the natural forces, or to pay for any natural product. This principal of limitation to private property in land, or reduction to the same status as personal property, can be effected without any derangement of business, or individual distress. Let such repeal or change of the law be prospective. After a certain date let no title be recorded which does not specify that said tract is within the prescribed limit, and is only required for occupancy and cultivation by the owner personally. Let such repeal have no effect during the life-time of present owners, who will be empowered to transfer their lands to persons only who with such transferred land will not have in excess of the determined limit. Let the executors, on the death of large landholders, have, say two years to make such disposal of the surplus, after heirs or legatees are secured in their proportions under the limitation.

By such a change in the system of land tenure no wrong would be wrought to any, as a full generation would be required to complete it. It would secure the greatest benefit to all who desirous of making themselves independent homes, are capable of self-employment, and are willing to work. The use of the land belongs to the living, and the dead should have no extended control over it.

The general government cannot perhaps, carry out this reform to its completion, but it can, and indeed has already recognized the principal of limitation to the acquirement of the public land as under the Homestead Act. Had that Act been framed in accordance with our recommendation and been carried out in good faith, the interests of our country and the condition of labor here would have been greatly improved. The lands would have been taken up consecutively, so that the patient and industrious settler would always have been near to markets and all social and educational facilities. Railroads would have been built as fast as needed without subsidies, and without the revolting spectacle of corruption we now behold. Now we have immense tracts interposed between settlers and settlements, which renders acquirement under the Homestead Act most difficult, and keeps the homesteader ten to twenty miles away from transportation. The lands which were given these corporations under the flimsy pretext that they were a public benefit, are now held from the settlers at a price far above the price the Government asks for its remaining land.

Congress can at least undo some of its unfortunate work. It can put what yet remains unsquandered wholly under the operation of the Homestead Act. The grants made in betrayal of the trust which committed the patrimony of the coming generations to Congress, can all be declared forfeited, especially where strict compliance with the terms has not been observed, and where the land has not passed into the hands of innocent parties.

In view of the past, however, the outlook is not encouraging, that under the sway of parties, Congress will do anything but foster giant corporations, grant subsidies and shape legislation generally to favor capitalistic adventures who flock the lobby and cry "give! give!" but who are first to volunteer the advice that no legislation is required to protect or counsel the working man; that he has liberty of contract and full freedom to work and save and become a millionaire, and should ask nothing more; and that the only way in which the government can possibly benefit him is to secure capital and corporations in their monopolies by high tariffs, steamship subsidies, railroad grants and franchises, and priviliges to bankers to furnish a circulating medium, while keeping open the doors to the wholesale importation of the depressed laborers of all other countries.

[See testimony of Jay Gould and John Roach, recently given before this Committee.]

It will be well for us to reflect that we are rapidly pursuing the course which, though absorption of the lands, debased the citizenship of the Roman republic, and brought in the empire under the Caesars, nineteen hundred years ago. Unless the course is changed the indications are that ere the twentieth century shall have dawned an organized oligarchy will control our government wholly, or conspire for its overthrow. The heart sickens to contemplate the struggle which the misled people are certain to make to regain their sovereignty when they clearly see the peril in which it stands.

All which is respectfully submitted.

J. K. INGALLS, Secretary.

Mr. Blair, chairman of the Committee, in questioning me, enquired how the large estates, as those like Mr. Astor's wronged the workingmen? If they could not buy houses or lots to build houses on of Mr. Astor as cheaply as of other parties? I replied that they could not buy of him at all. That he bought real estate, but had none to sell, in the sense of parting with ownership. He had them to rent, or sell by the month or year on terms which would require in ten or twelve years their value to be returned to him, the property still remaining his; in twenty-five years, thrice their value; and in fifty years, when by Hebrew law, the Jubilee came and all land was freed and all debts cancelled, fifteen times the value would have been paid, and still the property would be Mr. Astor's.

I did not urge this as any fault of Mr. Astors, but only of our laws of tenure, which placed no limit to the acquirement of land and that it would probably be found that even Mr. Astor failed to avail himself of the full power of the situation.

CHAPTER XIV.

Following Mr. George came Edward Gordon Clarke, who, in "Man's Birthright" and "The People's Right to Wealth," gave the public "the logical and Mathematical extension and completion" of the theory of Progress and Poverty. Mr. Clarke's diagnosis leads him to regard two per cent. as Nature's indicated rent rate: to be gathered by government as a tax, to be applied to the support of government and the advancement of the well-being of the people. This two per cent. rate he bases upon the ordinary death rate of mankind, when every one has to give back to Nature for the use of mankind, whatever may have been held at the time of decease. They hold therefore a reversionary interest, which is simply a rent. "This rent," he says. "is a foreordained, definite collection, fixed in the frame work of nature."

Mr. Clarke divided wealth into two parts. "the property of Nature, that inalienable gift of God to all generations, and the value created by individuals:" doubtless meaning through labor. He disclaims for himself and for Mr. George the imputation of ever having "touched Metaphysics." Yet his base of contention is one of the most metaphysical phrases ever uttered by that prince of metaphysicians. Aristotle, and only paralleled by another phrase of his "Nature's abhorence of a vacuum." And the one is as appropriate in physics as the other is in ethics and economics. I pointed out in Social Wealth in chapter. "Taxation as a remedy" (1895) that this school of reformers were "ignorant of or else affected to ignore the 'law of use,' that the doing and enjoying of a use are logically inseparable." "That tax or confiscation so far from being in accordance with nature, was corrective and subversive of nature, and intended not at all to 'complete economical science,' but to correct nature's blunders. What neither seem to comprehend is that the civil power to collect rent, make compulsory exchanges and enforce unequal contracts, is the evil to be abated, and not the inability of nature to bestow her bounty as she desires, or to effect the equality she intends."

Why a "foreordained, definite collection," should be dependent on frail human legislation for realization requires for answer a profounder metaphysician than ever Aristotle thought of being. Mr. Thaddeus B. Wakeman suggested that M. Clarke had expanded George's single tax theory till he had exploded it, and there is certainly no reason why the increment from all sources of increase should not be taxed back, as well from trade, finance, superior capacity and strength, as from superior fertility of land, or a choice location for business or pleasure.

In 1889 I had first acquaintance with Hugh O. Pentecost, the erratic but talented editor of Twentieth Century. He had at first adopted Henry George's Single Tax theory; but on reading Social Wealth, had taken up the vacant land question in earnest. At this time also Mr. Thomas L. M'Cready had separated from Mr. George and joined the Twentieth Century staff. There had been much discussion as to the question whether, should abolishing vacant land ownership fail to kill rent, Single Tax would be right. Most of the dissenters from Single Tax being disposed to admit, that in such case it would be necessary as a means to remedy the evil. In December of that year I handed to Mr. Pentecost a paper assuming that, in the case supposed, rent would be proven economic, and therefore to be right, or like other economic quantities, capable of beneficient use and just appropriation. I then pointed out the distinction between economic rent, arising under equal freedom and equal opportunity and monopolistic rent enforced by denial of freedom and opportunity, through exclusion from the earth, and the natural resources and raw material available to industry. Mr. M'Cready attacked the position, showing on general principles that there could be no justification for rent, and that no such thing as economic rent existed at all. Not noting that I had stated that it was subject to the vibratory action, and sometimes plus and sometimes minus, he appeared to antagonize my position, since these quantities cancel each other, the mean being zero.

I had no difficulty in showing this, and that economic rent interest and profits originated in these different degrees of productiveness of differing soils and situations, ability to labor, to forecast the relations of supply and demand, and choose between immediate and remote satisfaction. Rent of land is what one rends or takes from the products over the consumption required to obtain them. IInterest is what is rended or rent from the fruits of labor in any field of activity, above the amount consumed. Profit is what is taken from commodities in process of exchange in excess of what is consumed in the process. Where there is no excess of products over consumption, there can be neither rent, interest or profit, nor motive to exchange.

It is therefore unquestionable that the increase, accumulation or whatever it may be called, is due to a single fact, that wealth has been produced beyond what has been consumed in the service. Under natural or economic law, this excess or surplus would belong to the one producing it, whether his labor were employed directly in actual production, in required transportation or in the necessary services in circulating and exchanging.

Mr. M'Cready was a man of remarkable qualities of mind and of heart. Many of his contributions were brilliants. His letter in Twentieth Century, May 15, 1890 from his garden is "a thing of beauty," a humorous sketch imagined between Dr. Lyman Abbot, Col. Ingersol, and M'Cready's colored man Lewis, who "worships a distinct and positive personality. He wears a beard." Sits on a great arm chair in a court paved with gold and precious stones, which appears a little hazy to Lewis who has never seen any thing resembling them but a few glass beads. He is certain that when he shall get there he shall have a gold crown, golden slippers, and have a golden jewsharp in his mouth. "The Colonel's deity, as I understand it is a simple non-existence—a bit of nothing surrounded by space. And the God which Dr. Abbott reverences is a cross between the two, distinctly personal as to his feelings, but remarkably indefinite in other respects." And he intimates that if they "could get together for a few hours and turn themselves inside out, each one of them might learn something. Meantime I would get out my garden tools, and worship God after my own fashion, by planting a row of beans. I do not believe in a God. I do not believe in no God. But I have a most abiding faith in God. And I hold this faith not because somebody else has taught me; but simply and solely because experience has shown me that with it life is possible, while without it life is impossible."

The Twentieth Century never made good the loss of this gifted and upright man. On receiving the news of his death I sent the following note to Mr. Penticost:

"I write to express my sorrow for the loss of your co-laborer, Thomas L. M'Cready. He was only known to me through the columns of the Twentieth Century. The void his dropped pen has made will be difficult to fill. I seem to miss him as a well known friend."

Other writers I esteemed in Twentieth Century, were sometimes those I had sharp controversies with. Hugo Bilgram, C. L. James, J. M. L. Babcock, Mrs. Imogeue C. Fales, Miss Baldwin, Mrs. Dietrick, John M. Campbell, Alfred C. Cross, A. P. Brown, J. W. Sullivan, Bolton Hall, Thaddeus B. Wakeman, Clinton Loveridge and others. Controversy with them turned mainly on freedom of unused land vs. Single Tax. Free Banking against Government Banking. Credit money against metallic or commodity money and as between Land Reformers and Finance Reformers, the question, which was fundamental in Social Science, the land or the money issue.

In reply to a number of articles as to whether freedom of issuing money would free vacant land, the following was published in Twentieth Century, July 24, 1890.

This question can only be determined when we have a clear comprehension of the causes which produce rent, interest, and speculative profits, and of the relations which these subversions of justice sustain to each other. The fundamental fact in each is the ability of man to produce, from the land, with the natural materials and forces, more than he consumes in a given period. By itself, neither land nor labor produces anything in an economic sense. Only the labor of gathering makes the spontaneous productions of the earth subjects of exchange. Labor of itself is abstract, produces nothing till it is applied to matter.

But since labor so applied can produce more things for human use than is consumed by the laborer in producing it, the result usually exceeds the "cost limit," and yields a surplus or "increase." This is the prime source of all increase over actual consumption, furnishes the only pretext at justification for rent, interest, or other form of exaction without equivalent servce, and is the only plausible ground on which trained ignorance or studied prevarication reared the now exploded theories of the "wages fund" and "iron law of wages;" as stupid as they were wicked.

When the laborer, in equal freedom, is able to possess this increase or surplus, he is in a condition to exchange on equal terms with the surplus produce of others; and whether this be on a basis of cost of production, will not matter, so long as the same rule applies to the respective exchangers. One cannot justly take the entire product of another's labor by simply repaying the bare cost, from his own.

What present methods mean is exactly this: a subverted exchange, in which the landlord, money lender, and privilege holder is able to purchase "the whole product of labor" by returning to the laborer its actual outlay, taking the entire surplus fruits of any work, in consideration of supplying or returning the necessary things consumed. What the ownership of man thus did for the slaveholder, vacant land does for the landlord, legal tender, coinage laws, and bank charters do for the money lender, and tariff laws, patent laws, etc., do for manufacturers and speculators.

Nothing has ever stood or does now stand in the way of equitable exchange but the senseless superstition that the increase or surplus produced by labor belongs to some one other than the worker who has produced it. Privilege to hold vacant land out of use is clearly the primal agency in compelling idleness and in perpetuating the poverty of the lowly. And we can never lose sight of this fact without peril to all humanity reform. It may appear desirable and feasible to get usury and trade profits first out of the way. Although resting substantially on the same ground, we should reflect that rent, interest, and profit each is based on a distinct legal device. To repeal or counteract any one of them therefore could not work the abolition of the others, and could only affect them remotely.

Mr. Bilgram, Miss Baldwin and Mr. Babcock think that the interest rate affects the rent rate. But in proportion to decrease of interest on money will be the increase of the price of land and the rent will be unaffected.

Mr. Pentecost seems to think that we might allow Government to have its legal tender, so that it "did not prevent Tom, Dick, and Harry from making money of their own," letting slip for the moment the fact that, while we have a legal tender at all, the debtor, pushed for payment, would be compelled to sell the money of T., D., and H., which he might hold, for what it would bring, and buy legal tender at the price put upon it by those who were able to lock it up.

Now, the point I wish distinctly to emphasize is this: The repeal of pernicious monetary statutes will relieve us only from those grievances which are distinctly financial. Their repeal can have no important effect on those statute-created monopolies, which abridge one's right to manufacture and sell; much less can such repeal affect in any favorable way those who are deprived of home and opportunity of applying their labor productively, and who have no security to give, however plenty money may be, or however low the rate of interest.

It could be wished that Mr. Babcock had given us some key to his conundrum, as to how free money could abolish rent, taxation of tariffs, patent rights, etc., under which the people suffer. So far as I know, the "vacant landers" are willing to unite in any feasible reform of the money legislation, when it means repeal, but they cannot patiently see the fundamental land question pushed aside for the sake of trying new experiments with legislative interference which have always had pernicious results, whether applied to pet schemes of making and issuing money or to "sovereign remedies" in manipulating the taxing power.

There was another who entered the field, Michael Fluescheim, a Swedish Socialist, a capitalist and proprietor of large Iron Works who accepted the Single Tax theory and other progressive ideas, with modifications of his own. He criticised some of my articles in the paper and suggested that I should read Mr. George's book on the Perplexed philosopher.

The following forecasts of the land question was published in Twentieth Century in response to criticisms from Mr. Flurscheim.

It would seem that a complete acquaintance with the past and present tendencies of human society, should enable us to foresee to some extent the character of future institutions. But imperfect knowledge of the sequences of social phenomena, and of the laws which determine the evolution of industry, lead us greatly astray in our estimate of the positive effects of arbitrary will, autocratic or democratic. This question of the ownership or dominion of land is the fundamental one in social advancement. Numerous theories, remedies, plans and schemes are offered as a solution of a problem, but partially understood. From absolute dominion, by the state, involving the state superintendency of all industry and denial of all individual property in land to "free trade in land," as proposed by the Cobden Club, with unconditional dominion to the highest bidder; in other words to a plutocratic regime, there are many steps and shades. Among these, land nationalization, and single tax are the least positive; yet they form the skirmish line of the advancing hosts of belligerent socialism against the equally belligerent individualism, to the great perplexity of Herbert Spencer. Their great strength, from a philosophic point of view, is their facility in substituting hypothesis for facts, equivocal terms for exact phraseology, and the use of different words with identical meaning to signify different things. To them monopolists rent and economic rent are without practical distinction; voluntary, and compulsory competition are one and the same; willing and forced co-operation are without a difference, and unlimited dominion of vacant land and "occupying ownership" mean but the same thing. On the other hand the single taxer, at least sees a wide difference between "unearned increment" or "income from the rent of land" due or prospective, and "interest on the money" for which the land has been sold or mortgaged. How can one fail to furnish deductions to order with such facilities, even without the habit of passing by all points telling against their remedy as of no practical consequence.

In a recent number of the Twentieth Century, in allusion to my "the two rents contrasted," I am asked without any notice being taken of one of the six plain and broad distinctions given, to concede the whole question at issue. It is assumed that there are three factors in production, labor, land, ("assistance of nature,") and "the co-operation of human society." It is also assumed or implied that justice requires the mutual product to be divided into corresponding parts, to the   individual worker the share due to his work if he wrought alone, which could barely subsist him at best; the ballance, nature's and society's shares, to the community.

The only interest the producer of wealth can have in these hypothetical shares is to see that his own product is not diminished to a moiety or less by the false pretenses preferred by some lord of privilege to personate both nature and society; so that both the laborer and the land may be robbed; the land of its fertility and the laborer of his product.

The idea that nature contributes a share, capital a share, and society a share, to the productiveness of labor, is but a conception of barbaric times, to justify invasion and the forcing of tribute. Following in the thought ruts of unscrupulous advocates of power, where, as Gibbon says "the steps are silent, the shades are almost imperceptible, and the absolute monopoly is guarded by positive laws and artificial reasons." Mr. Henry George, after repeatedly declaring that "the factors of production are dual, not tripartite," thinks he finds "a distinguishing force, co-operating with that of labor," and hence that "it is impossible to measure the result by the labor expended," but "renders the amount of capital and the time it is in use, integral parts in the sum of forces," and so infers economic interest as well as rent. Now whether there are two, three, four or five factors, seems a matter of little account to him, so that he can avoid the intellectual effort of getting out of the time-worn ruts. The too utter stupidity of all these manufactured reasons for positing economic rent as other than an economic quantity, is seen when we notice that the shares of society, capital and nature are never claimed by their hypothetical ghosts, but by men who declining labor nevertheless seek a division of its earnings. Where nature's share goes to enrich her and increase her power, or the fertility of the soil, and where capital's share goes to furnish new plants and extend employment. no worker is wronged, no industry plundered or hampered. A passion not for the enjoyment of equal freedom, but for dominion over the places and productions of others, generates invasion and meddlesome interference. It is not the Scottish crofters, but Mr. Winans who stands in the way of industry, and causes all the crowding of one upon the other. When the salts and gases nature has lent to production are returned to her, her claim is satisfied. Her forces are persistent, her energy inexhaustible. When the plant is kept good, and increased as needed, capital's share is consumed.

But society's share? Co-operation of labor doubtless gives larger production; but to whom is this due? To those who "work together" or to those who have declined to co-operate, barred the paths of industry, and deprived labor of opportunity; withheld the earth from man and blocked the wheels of progress in every serious struggle? Yet these are the parties who now reap the unearned increment, and receive the rent, and to whom government renting or confiscation of rent, will award shares, and to the idle vagrant, as to the wealth producers, who so far have shared only bare subsistence.

Mr. F. in a friendly way asks me to concede the whole question as to the permanence of economic rent, and could he assure me in certain points as to the nature of the government leases, and that his premises were not mere shadowy hypotheses, I should be glad to please so courteous an opponent. That economic rent would increase under government control or under single tax, with unlimited leaseholds, forceful collection of rents, and remain undistinguishable from rack rents however "immense," I have not the least doubt. But that the condition of labor would be improved by such renting or taxing, my reasons for doubting will be given directly.

I am told "we can claim all that part of our produce which we obtain without being in the way of others, i. e., by barring their access to natural opportunities." But why protect any one in forcing such privilege? If the two can agree why should society interfere? Is it the home and tilled acres, of the occupier, or the landlord's dominion of vacant land that bars out labor from all opportunity? What but privileged monopoly stands in the way of each one having as much as he desires, or can rationally occupy, without disturbing others? No attempt is made to prove such necessity yet he says government can not be justified in interfering until such exigency arises. It would have been to the point to show that any man would be wronged or crowded because he could not occupy and use the same land at the same time that another did. Where is there the pretence that such a thing is probable? Ricardo's theory has collapsed; not only failing to account for the cause of rack rent, but to show that economic rent is a permanent quantity, which economic law cannot equilibrate. The Malthusian theory of population is dying of age. The later decades of this century show a narrowing of the increase in the birth rate, in all civilized societies, even in this youthful and bountifully land endowed nation, while in some it has reached its maximum, or is already on the decline. But suppose it were otherwise, and that increased population made access to land more and more difficult, instead of rendering the necessary quantity for one's support constantly less and less? How can renting of government or confiscating rent, increase the amount of land or diminish population, or even improve the disposition of those who seek to invade one another's domicils? Ricardo and Malthus treated British land ownership as an "Order of Nature," or a conferment of "Divine right." No idea of common or joint property as a personal right was conceived by either of them. Unless a man has a normal right (if only that of might) to private ownership of his person, the space necessary to be in and the surroundings necessary to life, then he must obtain or assume to have obtained by tacit social compact, the right of property in himself, and to room and opportunity to labor, because, two persons cannot occupy the same space or belongings at the same time, any more than can two atoms. But Mr. George is not in a position to profit by Mr. Spencer's perplexities. Mr. Spencer has reached a forecast which certainly justifies a "perhaps" or a "possibly," while the end to which Single Taxers deem social evolution tending is simply an impossible one. The primitive "communal ownership," from which "tenancy in common," in English law had its source, and of which "joint tenancy" was a variation, is the earliest and crudest form of land ownership in social life. The tendency to change to separate and private ownership of land was developed soon after property in movables arose, and gradually grew into extended domain, without intelligent limitation to check its encroachment on popular rights and invasion of the persons and properties of individuals. Nor has property in land, by our laws at present any restrictive conditions, such as attach to property in movables. To forecast progress, indicating no improvement, in human conditions, is to discredit the experience of the ages. From their own showing, it does not appear that single tax or even land nationalization can improve industrial or social interests. With the limitation of leases suggested by Mr. Alfred Russell Wallace, some improvement in human affairs might possibly be realized; but I know of no single taxer of note who accepts the idea. Mr. Flurscheim indeed speaks of "certain restrictions," but gives no hint as to what they should be. Without positive "limitation of estates in land" to "occupying ownership," either plan would only facilitate the reduction of the land and all productive property to a state of commercial monopoly. For two or three centuries, the regime of feudal ownership has been quietly changing from militant land dominion to the feudalism of trade. Landed property is no longer the inheritance of "an order of nobility," with its laws of primogeniture and entail; but has been absorbed by capital in its extension of dominion over the entire field of human activity. With or without remuneration to landlords, national control would be a surrender of all wealth producing industries to be capitalized; since a monopoly of leases, of unlimited quantities of land would enable all agricultural business, and all home-making to be put in trust, as other businesses are being.

The land of this country was from the first, national or common domain. The nation has sold it and given allodial titles. Only by exercising the right of eminent domain, can a rod of it be lawfully taken, and only for strictly public use. Only state socialism could reach the desired end, and which would prove a subversion of our political system. But suppose it otherwise? There would be not a possibility but a great certainty that it would again pass to private control through treachery of public officials as before.

With unlimited leases to the highest bidder, no poor man could obtain land, all rents would be monopoly rents, and workers must remain the serfs of those who had money to forestall possession, as in barbaric days the weaker was forced to leave the land or accept involuntary servitude. He had the "right of trial by combat," the measuring of arms and swords or bludgeons. Bidding on unconditional leases will give us the trial by measurement of purses, (unless we have a friend at court), with a tolerable certainty of being forced into involuntary idleness. This conflict will not be a struggle for the occupation of the best land, but for any land however poor, or situation however mean, and to retain the humble home one has toiled to rear and beautify.

But all this has "no practical bearing," with our theorists With the capture of the economic rent, things will go on swimmingly! But how! The difference between a deed and a lease is only one of time. A lease is a deed of sale of the use of land for one year, or one hundred years. (The shorter the time the worse and more hazardous for the occupier). A deed allodial ownership, is a lease of the same use "forever." The unconditioned lease increases the facility for engrossing through the law of the market the business of land speculation, as buying on margins facilitates stock speculation. The government would doubtless get the economic rent, which will prove a plus and a minus quantity. The successful leaseholder will have the monopoly rent, which will prove a wholly positive, and with all industrial progress, a constantly increasing quantity.

"But (says Mr. Flurscheim) if the reform will increase the worker's wages five fold, it must increase the economic rent," See! I see. Leaving out the significant if, it seems necessary to remind our friend that productive labor gives the only fund from which rent or taxes can be paid. So if the laborer's hire is multiplied by any ratio, great or small, the rent taker's and tax eater's income must be divided by a corresponding ratio. The plus of the worker's will thus be quite balanced by the minus of the rent gatherer's end of the economic scale. With considerable pertubation, no doubt, the librating tendency will as certainly be developed, as that water will seek its level from any external disturbance.

Shall we never be able to have it understood that the laborer does not suffer seriously because the best land and the first (or even second or third) class opportunities are closed to him, but because all land and all opportunities are barred by unconditioned deeds which do not differ in their operation from unconditioned leases. Had the bars best be taken down think you or shall we attempt to do what nature readily does when let alone, to librate incidental inequalities by stationing a government agent at the gate to collect the admission fees to the economic show? This will certainly benefit the showmen and the boodlers of politico-commercial combines, but would be carrying us backward to premedieval times, with the ancient tax-farmers, masquerading as landlords. I recognize no sign of progress in the wish to substitute bureaucratic for pluto-aristrocratic toll gathers. It is now the unconditioned dominion "over earth and man" which invades freedom and "gets in the way of workers." The depredations on commerce are not less, now that the agents of government "sit in the seats of customs," than when the buccaneer collected them on the high seas, or when the ancient baron fortified the mountain pass, and gathered tribute of every traveler.

I have not read "Social Statics" since its first appearance, more than forty years ago. Patrick Edward Dove's book was republished in this country about the same time. I found in the latter the anticipation of Henry George', entire land and tax scheme, and the identical course of reasoning by which he buttressed his "sovereign remedy." It then appeared to me a quack remedy, although a lucid diagnosis of the disease. As to Spencer's book, I have a vivid recollection of his imaginary talk with the backwoods squatter on unused land, and how the "man of straw" he set up to show off his intellectual prowess, floored the philosopher in the first syllogistic round, and of course, with the very words which the latter, thorough his English love of fair play, had felt compelled to put into the mouth of his lay figure. With a dumb antagonist, however, he was able to regain his feet, and ultimately silenced his speechless opponent by arguing of "absolute right;" although as a philosopher, he only made the squatter urge a relative right. He had found the land unused, had worked it without complaint from any one, and thought he had a better right to hold it than any man or any collection of men had to take it from him. It seemed to me then and did after reading "Progress and Poverty," that the man of straw had much the best of the argument. And Mr. Spencer himself now appears to think so. With his motive in expressing his perplexities I have nothing to do. We are all too ready to impugn the motives of opponents. Their facts and logic we cannot scrutinize too closely. To Spencer's ob-

jections to land-nationalization and state Socialism, I have seen no
convincing answer, from any quarter. Neither he nor his critics appear to recognize any alternative other than unconditional communal ownership of land, on the one hand, and unlimited private
dominion on the other. Either of which renders freedom impossible.
Standing between these however, is private "occupying ownership."
Had Mr. Spencer observed this, he would have reached a conclusion
satisfactory to himself and one requiring no "possibly" or "perhaps."
He failed by side-tracking, at its last stage, his own train of thought.
He says: "As the individual, primitively owner of himself, partially
or wholly loses ownership of himself during the militant regime, but
gradually regains it as the industrial regime developes, so possibly
the communal proprietorship of land, partially or wholly merged in
the ownership of dominant men, during evolution of the militant
will be resumed as the industrial type becomes fully developed."

In point of fact, the ownership of persons through conquests in
war, and purchase in trade, has under the industrial regime at
length resolved itself into an ownership limited to one's self.
Analogy would require then that the primitive ownership in land the
right of domicile appropriate to the use of the individual being lost
under warlike dominion, would be resumed under industrial rule,
and perfect the worker's ownership of himself and of his environment: the community also regaining its eminent domain over unused
or co-operatively used land, while the quality of private property
would only attach to that exclusively occupied in person. Mr. Spencer is doubtless correct in supposing that private property in one's
person and in the product of one's labor will continue to grow more
and more sacred. He is astray when he says that property in land,
not being a thing produced by labor, will in the future be held less
sacred than now. He wholly misses that portion of land which becomes private property by its relation to the laborer. He is right
doubtless as regards dominion of land, which involves subjection of
labor whether by the capitalist, feudal lord or state. This must necessarily disappear under equal freedom, or our era of industry retrograde to barbaric slavery or savage vagrancy. That property in
land, which labor has created by co-operating with and moving it to
productive use, will also without doubt grow to be held more and

more sacred, as our industry develops and as distributive justice becomes the watch-word of a higher civilization. Then and hardly till then will the forms of co-operation best suited to the times and the people, have fair play, or indeed any opportunity of trial. Nothing can be done in that direction while the great mass of the co-operators are landless and homeless. Without the earth for a fulcrum, the hypothetical lever of the reformer is powerless. Intelligence, not blind will, it is most probable under equal freedom, will render co-operation, communism and other forms of industrial life voluntary and rational, without awakening the barbaric desire of the one or of the many to force companionship or crude purposes on any. When the bars are taken away, rack rent will cease and economic rent will be set free. This will secure the occupation of the best places, and the working of the best fields by the best methods of co-operation. The worker will no longer seek the protection of the military power, against himself, nor shirk or shrink from mutually beneficial efforts. It is difficult to conceive of a positive or increasing rent requiring forcible libration, or such as is available for taxation, when only about ten per cent. of our land (exclusive of Alaska) is in any use, whatever and the most of that is second or third class. The best sites in cities and for cities are in the same ratio, kept out of use by usurpation, not by individuals getting in each other's way.

To this communication he only responded by a personal letter; saying in substance, that the time of action had come, and the time of theorizing and discussing doctrines had passed. He was on his way to Kansas and Topolobampo and debate must give way to work. How he emerged from the enterprise, I am not informed. If Mr. Owen and a few have made well out of it, certainly, many have sacrificed health, and whatever they took into the movement, and also their lives. I see yet nothing to change the view I expressed in the above communication, to which I came more than forty years ago, that industrial freedom was essential to any intelligent and successful enterprise in the direction of Social and co-operative industrial organization.

CHAPTER XV.

In addition to what I have stated in respect to my Tempreance experience and work, i should have mentioned my acquaintance with Dr. Jewett an early advocate of the cause, a very eloquent and efficient worker, Wm. S. Balch, and a number of clergymen of different denominations. Personally I had taken little active part in the movement, until 1841. The Whig Presidential campaign of 1840, with its "Log Cabin and Hard Cider emblems, had greatly loosened the popular conscience upon the temperance question, and wrought habits of inebriety and dissipation in both city and country. From this general relapse a reaction took place, finding especial expression in the Washingtonian movement, inaugurated in Baltimore by John Hawkins, and a few self reformed drunkards. I was living at Southold at that time, and had witnessed the orgies of the political campaign of the year before. Although opposed at first by the respectable and over pious, it appealed directly to the popular heart and carried all before it. Rich and poor, Whig and Democrat, pious and impious people came together animated by one purpose to stop the drinking habit. Total abstinance, from all intoxicating liquors became the battle cry, and an era of success was then attained without parallel in the history of the reformation. The north branch of east Long Island, which separates Peconic Bay from Long Island Sound, extends from Riverhead to Orient Point some 30 miles. Between the two Greenport is situated, and several villages; Jamesport, Franklinville, Aquebogne, Mattituck, Cutchogue and Southold. Within a year, this whole community was united as one in requiring the cessation of liquor selling, and the practice of temperance. The Tavern keepers at each of these places had licenses and claimed they could not maintain their places without the liquor profit. It was arranged that we should hold meetings at short intervals at each of the places and give the public houses the benefit of a dinner. In this way we prevailed upon them one after another to cease selling liquor, and give a pledge to that effect. Out of nine this pledge was kept, with tolerable exactness, with one exception for more than a year, and the first signs of breaking were on the part of those who had urged on the work as a public good, while keeping liquor in their homes, and in indulging in its use privately. Re-action from the state of tension came after a while, and some returned to their cups again when the stress of public sentiment was relaxed. But a considerable number of the reformed men, stayed reformed, and led sober and industrious lives. Engaged in this work were several men of mark. Dr. Frank Tuthill and a law student named Huntley, of Greenport, Dr. James Richmond of Southold, Revs. Mr. Beers of Riverhead, and Alonzo Welton of Southold, orthodox; Joseph Henson, Methodist, and Giles Waldo, who was teaching the academy at the time. All were effective speakers and workers. Mr. Welton was a fluent and attractive speaker, but had a weakness for the "last word", which is slanderously said to be a woman's peculiarity. He seldom allowed our village meetings to be dismissed without closing remarks, which left their impression on the minds of the hearers as they went away. This became "a little monotonous," after a while, and some of the speakers had expressed opinions in regard to it, particularly Mr. Huntley of Greenport.

Preparation was made for a Washingtonian celebration on 22d February, 1843 at Orient, and Mr. Welton and myself were invited to give addresses, together with Mr. Huntley, Mr. Beers and others. There was no railroad then, and I had no horse, and there seemed no probability that I could go; and so made no preperation for speaking. A friend from Cutchogue, who had been disappointed by a companion he had expected, drove up in the morning and insisted I should accompany him. Making hasty preperations I went. We arrived at Orient just as the procession was entering the church. Mr. Huntley immediately came to me saying that the committee had arranged, regardless of his protest, that Mr. Welton should have the last speech; but hoped I would be able to thwart him. The committee on speakers came to me as we had taken our seats on the platform, stating that there were three speakers to precede me, and Mr. Welton, who said he had come unprepared, would make a few extemporaneous remarks at the close, if it were necessary to detain the audience. I explained to them that I had not expected to come, and was wholly unprepared; that they knew I usually wrote out my remarks, and positively declined to speak at all. The opening services commenced, and every thing went smoothly on, until the three speakers had spoken, and the choir were singing the song following the last speech, when Mr. Welton coolly stepped down from the platform and walked out of the church. As the singing ceased, one of the committee came to me and stated the dilemma. Mr. Welton had left and they had just received a message from the hotel that dinner would not be ready for nearly an hour; that the audience must be held or they would not wait for it, and so the meeting prove a financial failure. He insisted that the audience were very desirous I should speak. Not wishing to be thought obstinate, I attempted an extemporary address, succeeding tolerably well. After speaking five minutes or so, I noticed a gentleman walking up the aisle and who took a seat upon the platform, appearing to pay close attention to what was being said. It was Mr. Welton. I continued to speak for a half hour or more; after which another song was sung, when Mr. Welton arose and prefaced his remarks, thus: "When the finest chords have been untouched by a master hand, it ill becomes one like me to take up the theme and assume to hold your attention;" and went on to say that it was necessary to entertain them a little longer, and after the fine speaking they had listened to he would attempt to "gather up the fragments, that nothing be lost." He then proceeded to pull out of his pocket a written address and read for a full hour; until the dinner, which it was feared would not be done, was in danger of getting cold, and some of the hearers went away with "last impressions" not altogether complimentary to the Rev. speaker.

On going to Danbury, I followed up the temperance work speaking often at their weekly meetings; and lecturing at Newtown, Stepney, Hattertown, Bethel, Beaver Brook, North Salem, etc. in the vicinity. And on my return to Long Island, continued to advocate total abstinence; going to Utica to attend a temperance convention, where I became acquainted with the veteran temperance reformer, Rev. A. B. Grosh. But after the movement degenerated into a political organization and sought to promote temperance and coercive measures and abandoned moral for legal suasion, I lost my interest, not in the cause of temperance, but in the irrational methods by which it was attempted to realize it. As my views of government became clearer, I thought less and less of its interference, in temperance, religion and morals; and came to regard license in any form as a most vicious proceeding. As to many prohibitionists, between license and free trade in Rum, the latter seemed preferable. But what estranged me most from the temperance movement was its evident tendency to join hands with the "God in the Constitution" party in attempts to subvert our ideas of liberty and establish a hierarchy for the control and government of our people. In 1888 I sent an open letter to Mrs. Clara B. Colby, editor Woman's Tribune, addressed to Miss Frances E. Willard. It was published, Mrs. Colby noticing it editorially in the same number as follows:

Away out in Idaho a fellow-traveler asked the writer the meaning of her badge, and when told he replied: "Oh, I thought it meant that you belong to the party that want to put God in the Constitution." This is but an illustration of a wide spread fear engendered by terms used by the W. C. T. U. at their conventions. And because this fear, or vague sentiment exaggerated and embodied by prejudice into a tangible danger, does exist, the Tribune publishes the letter of Prof. Ingalls, which shows very fairly and candidly how the attitude of the W. C. T. U. is regarded by many, and also makes very clearly all the points of persons who are opposed to anything looking towards a possible union of church and state or the introduction of a religious test of any sort. The Tribune hopes that Miss Willard, after the political campaign is over, will find time to present an answer to this letter which will give her own position and serve as a line and plummet by which to determine the value and meaning of convention phraseology.

AN OPEN LETTER.

To Miss Frances E. Willard:

Dear Madame:—It is with some hesitancy that a comparative stranger addresses you in this public manner; but one as prominent as yourself before the country, will not, I trust, deem it an intrusion, since my motive is to draw your serious attention to questions of human interests and duties, in a field where you have wrought with great zeal and effectiveness.

Recently, however, for some utterances of yours, or of those allied with you, your position, politically, has been severely criticised, particularly by correspondents of The Woman's Tribune; and although Mrs. Gage may be hasty and inconsiderate, I still think you will be held responsible for the conclusions she so summarily draws, unless you shall: as I hope you may, fully define your aim and purpose in regard to the principles of government, now being discussed both by the National and Prohibition parties. Your well-attested piety and devotion to the religion you profess, could be safely relied upon in any question of morals or religion, as such; but when a question of subjecting others to our will is involved, these qualities instead of giving assurance, but excite the apprehension of cool and considerate minds; for they reflect that the piety of "Saul of Tarsus," did not restrain, but stimulated him to hunt and persecute those who disagreed with him in religion; thinking he was doing "God's service." Thomas de Torquemada was a most devoted and pious Christian and so was Cyril, bishop of Alexandria, that "fierce hater of heathens and heretics," who caused the immolation of Hypatia, one of the most noble and pure of womankind, and in a manner so revolting to decency and so fiendishly cruel as to scarce have a parallel in the whole history of religious persecutions.

The power to interfere with the exercise of the individual conscience, once granted, and superior piety and a deep sense of religious duty make more imperative the purpose of coercion and despotic rule. The great and good Aurelius, was incited wholly by his piety and the desire to do what was best for his people, to the persecution of the early Christians. Europe to-day stands tremblingly apprehensive of a general war and a more despotic rule, because the present Emperor of Germany is known to be devoutly orthodox.

To me it seems due to the liberal minds interested in the several reforms you so ably champion, that a clear definition should be given to such phrases as: "God is the source of all power in governments." "It is the right of Christ to rule the Nations," etc. You cannot be allowed to follow the line of ecclesiastical subterfuge, which "palters in a double sense" through use of equivocal terms, however unintentional on your part this may be done. Should I use the term "government of God," I should mean the inevitable sequence of results to action in every cognizable domain of His Universe; and this implies the absence and denial to any man or woman of the right to control and rule any other man or woman, except such as the force of truth and the suggestion of worthy example cause them to voluntarily yield. But this is not the church's meaning of these phrases. She means a government under authority of a revelation made to barbaric people in ages long gone by; when authority was everything, exactness of statement of little account, man nothing and woman less—the slave of a slave or "the instigator of the devil to lure men to sin." She means government by "a visible head or vicegerent." Is it possible that this is the meaning you attach to the phrase? "The reign of Christ" is no less ambiguous. Is such confusion of language necessary in the honest statement of any important truth? I would define the last phrase to mean a "rule of equity" accepted through a love and free choice of the good, by mankind, and which all coercion must tend to prevent and frustrate.

I deem this, so far as we know, to have been the conception of Jesus, when he said: "My kingdom is not of this world, else would my servants fight." He aspired to rule the willing hearts of men. Any other rule, not strictly parental, is despotism, and can only beget hypocrisy or slavish fear; never trustful obedience.

Now the platform of the Prohibition, and of the National party, to both of which the W. C. T. U. is allied, in direct issue with our "Declaration of Independence," asserts that "governments derive their power from God," and not "from the consent of the governed." And here is met again the double meaning clericalism so delights in, for it may mean the denial of all power among men to legislate for mankind, leaving everything to the operation of God's laws in Nature, or it may mean a God-appointed hierarchy to interpret and enforce the law, as it is found in the old and new Testament, in the traditions of a church; or it may be the Koran, or book of Mormon, according as the followers of either might be found in a majority in any community. In the usual church meaning, this declaration is treason in every sense in which such term is applicable in our system of government, except by the actual "levying of war." So far as you are personally concerned, I think you sincerely desire the rule or reign of "One who cometh to judge the earth in righteousness," "rule in equity;" and promote the enjoyment of all in the reaping of the results of their labor—giving "to every man (or woman) according to his work;" and by no means, to enthrone brutal force, and carnal, murderous weapons for effecting spiritual aims. Certainly farther experience in that direction cannot be required. For the past is strewn with the wrecks of Nations and institutions which have attempted to make men moral, temperate and pious by coercive measures. To see how cruel such rule has invariably become, we only have to refer to that of the church, in suppressing the Albigenses, the Waldenses, and in plotting and completing the ruin of the Italian Republics of the 16th century. We need not indeed go out of our country and its colonial history in the days of Cotton Mather and the Puritan clergy of Massachusetts, whose deeds of cruelty and blood she can never erase from her record. Then suffrage if not confined wholly to the male citizen was confined to the church members. I shall not believe you would advocate such a curtailment of the franchise, unless you so expressly stated; but it would doubtless relieve many anxious minds, who are interested in your work as well as in the suffrage question, to have an explicit denial of any such purpose.

What the Christ enshrined in your affections seeks, as to these issues, we have no means of knowing, but as revealed by yourself. The desire to see love and justice reign may make you impatient of the slow progress of the world's reformation; but it must be borne in mind that the universe is run on a broader gauge than our finite minds can compass. In the absence of any proof that God and Christ have authorized any other means of reform than through man's appreciation of good, and personal experience of the results of his action, it seems to me the very height of presumption and blasphemy for any however good or great to attempt other means. Only what is most suspiciously miraculous, can be appealed to by the modern or ancient church to sanction the remotest authority to trifle with the freedom of man or woman, or interfere in any way to lessen their individual responsibility. God has never directed the creation or destruction of any forms of government, but has left us free to learn by trial which is best suited to any times or peoples. God does not enforce virtue, temperance, or piety, but by allowing us to learn by experience, "what is good." For more than fifteen centuries the church, however, has been trying the alternative of force and superstitious fear, and of course has failed in employing the Divine sanctions of reason and experience; inculcating instead, hatred of differing opinions and bending all moral axioms and aims to increase her authority and maintain her power, over the actions and beliefs of men. To do the best one can, without conforming to her behest, "is sin." To follow her direction, and accept her terms turns the foulest guilt to grace. All this is very churchlike; but certainly not God or Christlike, in any sense you usually employ those terms.

Now the application together of these widely diverse principles, to temperance or morals of any kind, is simply impossible. The good which the laborers of the W. C. T. U. have effected in this direction, have been largely counterbalanced by the spirit of partisanship and intolerant zeal evinced in ways which the "Divine Government" has never instituted and Jesus never sanctioned by word or act; resulting in espionage and detective work, perjury and betrayal of confidences such as can only be justified by the church casuistry, that "the end justifies the means." For the man coerced to virtue is vicious still, and only flatters with hypocrisy till espionage is withdrawn. This is proven by the history of the temperance reform, with which I have been acquainted almost from the inception. After an erratic experience of about a quarter of a century, it had so failed as to offer no serious opposition to the orgies of dissipation attending the "hard cider" campaign of 1840. At its close John Hawkins and other self "reformed drunkards" began the Washingtonian movement. They were not Christians in the church sense, nor political partisans. Eschewing politics and sectarian religion they were given a cold shoulder by the formally religious. At first it was with difficulty that a church, vestry or school house could be obtained for their meetings. But the intrinsic merits of their reform soon gave it power, and shortly marked one of the eras of sobriety and abstinence in our Nation. As soon, however, as it became popular and they saw the car moving, the clergyman, the lawyer, the politican and physician concluded they had best get on and ride. The first saw that his religion was necessary to make men truly temperate that without grace temperance would be counted sin. The lawyer discovered that the important thing to do was to "make a law," in order to give their cause success. The politician espied a place in which he could work his "caucus" and "political deal." Even the doctor discovered something advantageous to his craft, and suggested the substitution of the apothecary for the dram shop, and, in the language of a regular M. D., insisted that there should be required "a physician's prescription, in place of the dangerous exercise of private judgment in regard to stimulants required by the laity."

"If you desire to become temperate," said the ecclesiastic, "ask the church, accept its creed and become pious." "To remedy this evil," said the attorney, "make a law that I may interpret and enforce."

"You can only accomplish your aim," said the office seeker, "by political action."

"If you must drink," said the doctor, "the only safe method is to have me prescribe it."

The Washingtonians replied: "We are here to do what you have ever left undone, and to reform an evil, which your callings separately or collectively, have never corrected, even if they have not made it worse."

But in the end formalism triumphed. Betrayed by a few weak but eloquent men, like John B. Gough, the good work, so nobly begun, became a semi-religious movement loaded with little ambitions and jealousies of clerical, legal, political and medical professionals. At times the true reform spirit has been revived only to be betrayed as before.

It is due to yourself, and also to the movements with which you are associated to say that your work seems largely to partake of the true humanitarian spirit. I greatly admire your way of putting the question of prohibition: "each to prohibit himself," and thus establish a government of self-control; a very different thing from having a government for everybody by someone! Admitting what is yet unproven, that "protection protects,' 'and "prohibition prohibits," who shall protect us against our protectors, and prohibit the prohibitors? The church uses fermented wines in the religious service. Physicians prescribe alcohol ad libitum through the druggist, who is nearly as multitudinous as the rum-seller, and with the tobacconist is doing more to wreck the health and happiness of mankind than he. The wealthy import wines and liquors and drink at home and treat their fashionable friends. Will police supervision or suppression of the saloons, be effective, or appear to the many otherwise than as a measure creating invidious distinctions? The intemperance of the home of wealth, the fashionable hotel, and the exclusive social circle, is not reinforced from the low groggery and gutter, but directly the reverse. You seem to have already apprehended that, and hence the stand against the "high license" craze. You are correct in supposing "it is the rum-seller's profit, which sustains the deleterious traffic."

And it seems to me that the true basis of reform in all the social matters you are engaged in, is industrial and economic, and can be effected only through liberty, not repression; love, not violence; by means of equity and knowledge of exact truth, as it is found in the nature and experience of mankind and by promoting exact estimates of the value of things. The true home for which you mistakenly suppose we are indebted to the religion of the church, had its origin in the Human Nature developed in such freedom as existed under the Germanic tribes. The Hebrews and all polygamic nations had harems and seraglios but no homes, in the sense you mean; and the monogamic Greeks and Latins, with their loose sexual morality never reached your ideal; purity was demanded of the woman, but not of the man. The word home is Anglo Saxon, and is wanting in the languages of the east and Southern Europe. With her Christmas, and Easter, and many of her fasts and festivals Christianity derived her conception of the heimath or "home," and its faithful attachments to the women whom Tacitus and Pliny described. But our comercial proprietorship of the land makes to woman our modern home a mockery. When woman is "evicted" from home as our laws provide, she is unqueened, if not unsexed. Industry without opportunity or raw material, becomes enslaved to greed; and the man and the boy seek in the saloon, the satisfaction which a homeless shelter denies. The woman is reduced to drudgery, or seeks escape through dangerous paths, or becomes the victim of marital ownership to one perhaps whose inherited lands or annuities have enabled him to appropriate the earnings of others without contributing any useful service of his own. How widely different is the actual Christian home, especially of the industrious poor, from the one you have idealized? Not the children of the undevout alone become prey to intemperance and vice; but the most pious parents have children with wrecked lives. Vicious ways in youth, when not hereditary, are due to over-indulgence or unnatural repression, and in about equal degree to each. Mental indolence is the main source of error, and is fostered by yielding gratifications without estimating and exacting cost, or in suppressing normally healthful activities. The over-burdened and care-worn woman, whose mother-love is thus tried and sacrificed is in a condition to do both.

How little our popular religious teaching is calculated to correct these tendencies, or remove the fundamental injustice, no one can be better informed than yourself. The ecclesiastical or political machine does not seek the advancement, but the subjugation of the human being, of the woman particularly. It holds out the promise of an imaginary good, yet fails to encourage broad and varied investigation and experience in demonstration of what is good.

I can by no means close my eyes to the fact that religious bigotry and designing cabals in church and state are preparing to subvert such liberties as we now enjoy. "The Man of the Vatican" has never retracted his claim to make and unmake rulers of states. He prescribes to-day the manner in which citizens, who are members of the communion, shall exercise their political rights. When the question of church domination comes, absolutist in church and state will unite. Catholics will not all be found Romanist, then, nor Protestants all liberals. Reactionary Rome will draw to her side a large following from the Anglican church, particularly that branch of it, in this country, which still sighs for the return of monarchy, and a "Church by law established." The Episcopalian, including the Methodist and the Presbyterian, who is for state interference in matters of religion, will to a large extent be drawn into the retrograde vortex or will "pool their issues," and take the chance of obtaining or sharing supremacy. It is now evident that a despotic rule in state will make common cause with the religious hierarchy. Protestant England and Germany with their aristrocracies of birth and wealth are to-day in league with papal Rome to shut out progress and to suppress the discussion of the land question and other social reforms.

We can count, upon the other side, all friends of full religious toleration, the heretical sects generally, and all however orthodox who hold to congregational methods of church government. The Baptist rather than the Methodist should stand as a wall against any approach of concerted action between church and state, would they not shame their history and traditions and cover the names of their martyrs and honored leaders with ignominy. We need not flatter ourselves that this struggle is not coming, and soon. May it be not a bloody one like the issue of chattelism. But from such conflict only a love of good, exactness of knowledge, honest work and noble endeavor can save us.

The shallow device of the National party convention, in starting out with a denial of intention to join church and state, can deceive no one. They afterwards expressly proclaim it. It does not matter whether the church is united to the state, or subjected to it, as in England, where it is simply a political mistress. Again the state may be subjected to the church. Such a government Rome, Sicily and Italy had until united Italy displaced them. Can any well-wisher of his kind desire to see the return of such rule? "Most Christian" Spain is now burning Bibles and her church is openly advocating the re-establishment of the Inquisition so "that sinners and heretics may be adequately punished." Yet such is the inevitable issue of any government, under an organic law into which the name of the Incomprehensible is incorporated, as proposed by the National platform. It could only lead to a deadly strife between the sects for mastery of the state or a general "trust" of the hierarchies to rule by "divine right." To place the utmost charitable construction on this purpose would be to assume that it intends after all a popular government, not a hierarchy, in which the legislators, judges and executive shall be churchmen; but this would necessitate confining the franchise to the church membership. It would be a perilous as well as unjust thing to disfranchise thus a majority of present voters. But since women outnumber men in the churches and have not yet been enfranchised, they might submit to such limitation. I see that some of your public speakers and papers, are noticing, without disapproval the application of an "educational limitation" to the franchise for women, though no such limitation exists as to male suffrage.

But what I am nterested to know is this, whether your idea of a

"Godly government" contemplates issues of this kind? And if so, it seems but just that it should be clearly stated, and so be fully understood by such advocates of woman suffrage as Susan B. Anthony, Lucy Stone, Elizabeth Cady Stanton, Mrs. Gage, Mrs. Neyman, and a host of other pioneers and earnest workers, and by all who cherish the memories of Lucretia Mott, Ernestine L. Rose and Frances Wright.

It is proper I should add that I do not think it possible you can really intend anything of the kind; but it is evident that your position is otherwise quite misunderstood not by Mrs. Gage alone. The advocates of "a religious test" so regard it and quote you as sustaining their fanatical or designing aims. When the "impending crisis comes" I confidently hope you will be found upon the side of freedom, and that your persuasive voice and facile pen with all "sweet reasonableness" and "invincible purpose" will support the cause of human progress and point the way to "Reason, not to Rome." I am consoled, moreover, by the reflection that even if woman's enfranchisement should lead to the putting of the Awe-full Name into the Constitution it will be the "Elohim" of Genesis, the optimist God, who saw that everything he had made "was good," and not the "Jehovah" the pessimist "Lord God" of the "second mention," as Gladstone terms it, who saw everything evil, nothing he did not curse, even to the clod of "ground." Still I think it would be far better to incorporate the love and knowledge of good in our lives and thoughts, than to put any name however sacred into an organic law to be wrangled over, in the struggle for power between conflicting sects and factions.

With much respect,

J. K. INGALLS.

But more than eight years have passed away and no answer has been given to it though I have been informed that she promised a mutual friend to answer it. Rev. Jesse H. Jones of North Abington, Mass., requested the privilege of a reply; but Mrs. Colby deemed it Miss Willard's duty to reply to the questions propounded, and refused to admit a reply from any other party. Utterances from Miss Willard since, particularly one from England on the subject of general legislation on Temperance, and other subjects involving the in-

terference of the state with social and religious questions, indicate
too plainly, that she has cast her influence with the coercionists
and subversionists.

CHAPTER XVI.

It is proper that I should give some experiences with the
individualist group of the radical movement. I was drawn to the
teachings of Proudhon more especially by his stand upon the question
of interest, and so inclined to accept his theory of government, or
rather of no government. An elder brother of mine, Seth H. Ingalls,
had many years ago said to me: "There will be no tolerable condition for the people who labor for their living and no permanent success to the honest business of the country, as long as the power of
taxation is permitted to the government." I deemed this at the time
a saying too radical for serious thought but admitted that the taxing power should be more thoroughly defined than it ever had been
and narrowly limited. Somewhere about 1872 I became acquainted
with Benja. R. Tucker ,who subsequently published the Radical Review, in which was printed my essay on Work and Wealth, afterwards issued by him in pamphlet form. Since my first advocacy of
land reform, I had realized the necessity of urging it on rational and
economic grounds, rather than by inviting legislation to formulate
and enact statutes. The Land Limitation advocated by Mr. Evans
and his conferes, I regarded as a very rational method, since it
did not multiply or complicate the legislative function; but merely
applied the principle of "limitation to estates in land," which now is
without condition as to extent, or in its ability to deprive men of all
access to the use of elemental nature, essential to both life and liberty.

Mr. Tucker, who had absorbed Proudhon, in his early study of the
French, and translated his "What is Property," also his "Economic
Contradictions," subsequently started the publication of Liberty, a

paper devoted to Anarchy; not the Anarchy of John Most and the physical force propogandists, but of the scholarly and philosophic radical, who seeks to convince by logic and reason, not by force and outrage. He sought the patronage of the Land Reformers for his paper and to this end had an interview with myself, William Rowe, Col. Beeney, and others in New York. Our aims and measures appeared to coincide except in one point; that of asking legislation to limit the ownership of land. When asked by Mr. Rowe whether he would do this, he scornfully replied that he would not. He was asking legislators for nothing, but to stop their interference in human affairs. The others saw in this answer what I did not, that he was opposed to withdrawing from the landlord the power to exact rent. I saw that the abolition of law, not more law, was what was needed in land and all other reforms, and that his paper was likely to prove a most useful medium through which to proclaim the freedom of the earth to the use of Man. They became reconciled, and Mr. Rowe continued a hearty supporter of Liberty until his death, some ten years since, as did many others. Its eight or ten years of heroic struggle against most adverse conditions has fully justified my estimate.

In a letter to the 20th Century, giving some account of the early Land Reformers, I mentioned Liberty as having been a great help to me and to others, in enabling us to discharge our minds of the fallacy that political action, and the humble petitioning of government for the amelioration of human conditions was essential to the triumph of free land. On this I received a personal letter expressing his great pleasure at my recognition of the service Liberty had been to me in clearing my mind of the delusion that through statute law any substantial reform could be promoted.

While never identifying myself with any distinctive school of thought, and while seeing that government of some kind will get itself acknowledged and enforced until men are wise enough to do without it, I nevertheless think that the tendency now is greatly toward the increase of the rule of laws and of collective control, and that the conscientious reformer is likely to show himself upon the side of liberty, and the rule of reason, rather than the rule of force. When Mr. Stephen T. Byington, inaugurated the Anarchist Writing

Corps, I gave him my name as a member, without however subscribing to any creed, or to any essential doctrine of the anarchistic school; acceding only to the hypothetical "Equal Freedom" as the measure and standard of judgment in matters of social advancement or of industrial or commercial endeavor.

But with Mr. Tucker's admiration of Proudhon, he had imbibed a blind devotion of Proudhon's "Mutual Bank" hobby (and we all have hobbies) which the French philosopher had adopted as a means to right all wrongs to labor by uprooting the upas tree of usury, and which he deemed so important, that he would effect a bouleversement of the planet if necessary to accomplish it. How mutual banking is related to equal freedom any way other than is mutual insurance, mutual farming, mutual house-keeping, co-operative store-keeping, or co-operation in any field of production or exchange, neither M. Proudhon, Col. Greene nor Mr. Tucker or any of his disciples, who are many and able, have deemed it necessary to explain.

As early as 1888, in the investigation of Mr. George's method with rent, and his contradictory position on interest, the distinction between the terms under economic law, and statute law became apparent; and in a New York journal I made plain the contrast, showing that what arose as rent, interest and profit economically, was salutary and tended to equalize compensations, while that arising under conventional enactments was of the nature of tribute, and the principal cause of the unequal compensations obtained by useful labor, as compared with that obtained by privileged idleness and the scheming greed of those who were enabled by legal devices to avoid the necessity to work and thus escape the operation of nature's economic laws. I showed that the contention of the moralists of ancient and modern times was against the forced usury, law sustained. The interest, rent and profit which the economists endorsed was a wholly different thing. That what the latter approved the former did not condemn, and that what the former condemned, the latter did not approve. All forms of tribute and invasion are as much opposed to economic law, which has normal operation only under equal freedom, as to the moral law.

In 1889 I sent to Mr. Tucker the article following:

INCREASE: ECONOMIC OR TRIBUTARY.

To the Editor of Liberty:

For more than a half a century I have contended that rent, interest, and profits were wrong and should be abated. I had all that time a half-latent idea that something was lacking to an exact conclusion, and constantly anticipated having it pointed out to me; but no advocate of capital has ever done so. Through my own investigations, aided by comparing the pro and con of the discussion among Socialists. Single Taxers and Anarchists, I have arrived at the conviction that these forces, so potent in social and industrial life, are economic as well as monopolistic.

Economists treat rent, interest, and profit as if solely embraced within the principles of exchange. Moral, and, generally, religious reformers have classed them with the tribute-gathering of despotic power. Now from neither of those suppositions alone can any satisfactory conclusion be deduced, because the terms embrace wholly contradictory and incompatible things under the same name.

It has been suggested to me by Mr. C. L. James that this distinction has been noticed by Proudhon and also by Karl Marx; but he gives me no quotation or specific reference by which I can ascertain whether they also point out that, on their economic side, rent and interest are salutary as well as inevitable in their operation. All this may, perhaps, be inferred from the "Economic Contradictions" of Proudhon, but has he anywhere put it in clear form? If Karl Marx has his whole scheme of State Socialism becomes a complete non sequitur. For then it is economic law, not human misdirection and misgovernment, he essays to rectify and reform. I do not see either how Proudhon could demand the abolition of economic rent and usury. With the broad distinction between the economic and the monopolistic force involved in these terms, we have to notice the undulatory motion of the ratio of values, and the mean or point of rest. This mean, as I distinctly stated in "Social Wealth" and more fully showed in ' Economic Equities," is zero.

Economic rent is confined to the more fertile soils and the more eligible location. But the less fertile soil becomes the more fertile by a change of culture, discovery of new uses and new methods, and nothing is more fluctuating than the valuations of location, which a thousand incidents may reverse or change. In cities the relative value of location is one of constant variation. Advantage from use of capital is balanced often by glut in market. That from growth of animals and things is balanced by their subsequent decrease and decay. There is an appearance of increase when labor or care is bestowed on them in process of growth and of loss when bestowed on them in process of decay, and these on the whole, balance each other. That which is reaped as profit under our system of legislative interference is a wholly different thing, and results from class law. Rent of land is now tribute to privilege for the use of nature's forces and opportunities. Under a system of ownership where occupancy was the sole title it would disappear, and rent would then be a vibrating quantity, and subject to that modulating law which governs movement in every department of nature would secure always the cultivation of the best land. The grand distinction between the economic value and the monopolistic price of things is that the first constantly seeks the level, zero, from whatever cause of disturbance it may have become elevated or depressed, while the other forces an artificial level, as a dam prevents a stream from following its normal drift to the sea. Interest on money is held to a positive ratio, because of "legal tender" and exclusive currency laws, as well as by a monopoly of land, tariffs, patent rights, and other forms of privilege.

But the land, the plant, the stock, and even the currency require "care and keep," corresponding to, indeed constituting, the value of their use. Such service and such use are the complements of and balance each other. Demand and supply regulate the value of such service and use, the same as of other services and commodities, and constantly tend to bring them into equilibrium. Whenever stock is in excess, the service demanded for its care, or its conversion into more desirable or more durable forms, will command a premium. But such premium will tend to divert labor from other fields to this, until equilibrium is restored, after many vibrations in which will occur increased demand for stock and a premium for its use. This will tend to attract labor to lines most favorable to itself and to all. Herein appears the reciprocity principle between the use and the care of things. I have not space for further illustration. Care and use are exchangeable and therefore economic, and will bear alternate direct and inverse ratios to each other, as do other things exchangeable, the mean of which ratio is zero. That is, the service which does or procures the use will equal it in price, subject to the fluctuations from plus to minus, caused by the relative supply to the demand.

Thus a distinction conclusive of the incompatibility of economic with monopolistic increase is found in their different effects on equitable exchange. Variations in price do not involve permanent loss to any party. Prof. Summer attempts to emphasize the equities of trade by saying: "The earnings of commerce are not taken from that which any one ever had." I quote from memory. He wishes to be understood that the values added by commerce may be equitably taken by those who perform the services of commerce, and this is or would be true under freedom; but a patent untruth under the reign of privilege; for even he would not admit that prices under protective tariffs or government subsidies were other than robberies of labor. In rent and interest under monopoly of land and class currency laws the steal is still more certain and quite as apparent. It is only by the use of terms capable of such opposite meanings that legal monopolism is able to appear other than it is, an organized despoiler.

STATEMENT OF THE PROBLEM,—ECONOMIC.

Care and maintenance of productiveness=Use of land.

Service of superintendence and conservation=Use of stock, plant, etc.

Care in preservation from decay=Growth of things.

Labor cost of production=Mean prices of commodities. Cost is not the limit, but the mean of price.

STATEMENT OF MONOPOLY INVOLVED.

Rent=Privilege arising from monopoly of land.

Interest=Privilege from legal tender and currency class laws, giving a monopoly.

Profits=Governmental subsidies and protection from the economic law of supply and demand.

By their very terms these are excluded from any equation with values effected through labor.

I shall be glad to have these general propositions criticised, the more severely the better.   J. K. INGALLS.

Glenora, New York.

This he published, commenting upon it as follows:

Mr. Ingalls calls for severe criticism of the general propositions advanced in his article on "Increase." From Liberty he will certainly receive support rather than opposition, for it never entertained a view different from that which he now holds. If it has any criticism to offer, it is that Mr. Ingalls is not justified in claiming originality and novelty for his important distinction. Even those who seemingly dissent from his main conclusion and who insist that cost is the limit of price do not in reality mean to contradict him. From the standpoint of economic logic. Mr. Ingalls's phraseology is doubtless to be commended as superior in point of exactness and accuracy. But it should be borne in mind that, when Warren and Andrews spoke of cost as the limit of price, they did so because they aimed at emphasizing the ethical side of their doctrine and the contrast which equity presents to commercial cannibalism.   T.

Subsequently, I sent an article to Twentieth Century, showing six positive distinctions between the rent arising economically and that which sprung from legal privilege. On its appearance I received another personal letter from Mr. Tucker, characterizing the performance as splendid. It seems only gradually to have dawned on Mr. Tucker's mind that my contention about Interest and rent was dangerous to the claims of the Mutual Bank, for as late as 1894, in a discussion with Mr. Byington occurs this passage:

"It must not be supposed, however, that I share Mr. Robinson's view that economic rent is not a reality. I believe that economic rent exists now, and would under freedom, but then with a tendency to decrease and a possibility (though not a probability) of ultimate disappearance."

Had he considered that rent and interest were the same, and identical in their source and in their relation to the awards of labor, he would not in the same No. of Liberty with the above have contended that "free and mutual banking" will cause interest to "disappear as an influential economic factor." December 15, 1894 the following appeared in Liberty from me.

UNESCAPABLE INTEREST.

There is an economic interest as well as rent, and it differs from that which is captured by the stronger and more cunning from the weaker and more stupid through the enforcement of barbarous (not economic) laws and customs. Since the days of Jeremy Bentham, the nature of usury has been argued, pro and con, on parallel lines; neither party discovering that what he approved was not at all the thing which the other condemned. Neither traced interest to its source.

Interest is derived from the increase of any labor over its bare support; the natural wage of Adam Smith, where it exceeds the starvation wage of David Ricardo. For, without such increase, rent, interest, or profit could have no existence. Some labor, from unfavorable location, inefficiency, or lack of knowledge, is unproductive. In the application of new discoveries in machinery, and in new processes of production and exchange, and in opportunity to co-operate with others in effort, the one who holds to the old method works at a disadvantage in comparison with the one who first adopts them, and there seems neither utility nor equity in requiring the alert man to share his surplus with the laggard, as the State Socialist would recommend, and as the Anarchist must do before he can abolish economic interest.

In the recent discussion in Liberty more than one disputant follows grooves which prevent him from seeing the true position of his opponent. From the standpoint of the sentimentalist, interest is tribute captured from the increased wealth due to labor, by the help of State interference. But the economist sees the economic increase from successful labor, and thinks it just; and, whether just or not, it is unescapable,—not because, as he imagines, property is productive (unless, indeed, it is made to embrace the land or the laborer), but because of the uncertainty of all human endeavor, and because men are willing to pay a premium for the opportunities and instruments which best assure success, or the immediate gratification of desire. Now, that official circulating credit could eliminate the uncertainties and variability of productive industry is quite problematical. Could it affect the rate of interest in any way, it could not abolish it for the reasons given. That mutual banking, or freedom to engage in the issue of circulating credit, can eradicate usury has never been demonstrated or logically made to appear. The legal or market rate of interest is at present greatly increased by the charge for the endorsement of one firm by another. A premium of from one to three per cent., and even more, is voluntarily given to a party of well-known soundness by a party not as well known, though sound in point of fact.

Had each party the freedom to circulate their credit at will, it could in no wise alter this relation of the parties in such transactions. The credit more widely receivable would command a premium over that confined to a narrow and local circulation.

It is when contracted indebtedness is subjected to enforced settlement that the true inwardness of our governmentalism is manifest. In soliciting the State to collect his debts, however contracted, the Archist exposes his true position. But, when the Anarchist calls upon his comrades to help him enforce his contracts, because they are contracts, and assumed to be made under freedom, in what important respects does he differ from the Archist? To me it seems quite immaterial whether abundant money makes the rate of interest higher or lower, or whether a three-cent piece could do the business of the world,—as evidently it could, were it sufficiently divisible and all other money effectually prohibited. What utility requires is material, and whether the interest we are investigating is economic or the fruit of capture and exploitation. If economic, it is necessarily variable and undulating, and yet inexpungable. If exploitive, it is Archic and involves interference and physical enforcement.

Economic interest is inevitable from the uncertain award of labor in production and the variations in the ratio of supply to demand; besides, there is a large proportion of the laborers unable and wholly disinclined to employ themselves. This state is likely to continue for generations, and they will continue to sell their labor at a rate which will yield profit to the employer, out of which he can pay interest. Government might despotically attempt to prevent this by law, with punitive sanction; or by wholesale employment of labor, at no profit. How an Anarchist could imagine a scheme of circulating credit would obviate the defects of ignorance and negligence, and the variations of values in exchange, is too deep for me.

The importance of circulating credit, or of any credit whatever, except the unavoidable balances of reciprocal commerce, is greatly overrated by fiat-money men, and by paper-money men of all classes. All time credits, all loans on bonds, etc., are but compounding the penalty for deferred payment; are not only unnecessary, but vicious, with little compensative benefit for the incalculable harm they do. Even the Christian formula: "Lord, hoping for nothing again," proves oftener a curse than a help to the borrower. To discount the future results of one's labor can only result in loss. This is particularly true of the wage-worker, who finds himself often under the necessity of requiring his wages before they are earned. Neither government nor comradeship can usefully interfere here. The form or material of money can in no way change the relation between borrower and lender, unless, through contraction or inflation by those holding the authority, it is made to favor the one at the expense of the other, which violates both equity and utility.

The State, as an arbitrary potency, has created and sanctioned the appropriation of the land by private greed, and of the laborer as well; has devised for a class the monopoly of opportunities of production, exchange, and finance. To divest it of the powers thus used is the only logical plan for restoring economic equity. With the taxing power unrestrained, it can be exercised to the fattening of favorites by starving the laborer. It can tax the issues of your mutual banks out of existence, as it has already those of your State banks.

The operation of economic interest, as of rent and profit, tends to equilibrium, equality in compensations and of conditions. There is no occasion to antagonize it or decry it. Liberty has accorded to this theory of interest the merit of novelty. Will any of its writers or readers attempt to show that "what is new in it is not true?"

To this he replied that I had given no clear definition or measure of the term. He must know what was the poorest capital in use and how it was recognized as such, or "Mr. Ingalls' economic interest was a decidedly indeterminate economic factor." He offers no help in ascertaining the unknown quantity, or to the method of determining what is the poorest land in explaining economic rent; but insists on direct answers to three other questions, which he puts "straight-way:"

1. If a thousand men engaged in different lines of business unite to form a bank of issue; and if the bank of issue unites with other similar banks for clearing purposes; and if said bank lends its naturally well-known circulating credit to its members (or to others, for that matter) against conditional titles to actual and specific values given by the borrowers,—do these loans of the bank's credit cost the bank anything beyond the salaries of manager and assistants, rent of building, expenditure for paper and printing, losses by depreciation of securities, and sundry incidentals?

2. Do not statisticians and economists agree that a discount of one-half of on e per cent. covers the expenses referred to in the preceding questions?

3. If men were free to unite in the formation of such banks of issue , and subject to no penalty or tax whatsoever for so doing, would not competition between the banks thus formed force the price of the service rendered by them down to cost,—that is, one-half of one per cent.,—or to a figure closely approximating it?

Now, I insist, and I have a right to insist, that Mr. Ingalls shall answer these three fair and pertinent questions directly, without extraneous discussion, without any mingling of considerations or speculations not absolutely essential to the answers. For either these direct answers will be what I think they must be, and then the case of the Anarchists (so far as finance is concerned) is established; or else they will be something else, and then the case of the Anarchists falls. T.

In January, the controversy was continued:

NARROWING THE INTEREST ISSUE.

To the Editor of Liberty:

To the three questions propounded to me in your issue of December 15, I make answer and say:

To the first: That the loans of the banks supposed would cost them nothing but running expenses and incidental outlays and losses. But such banks are only possible under the three conditions mentioned, neither of which is supposable without a motive to derive some profit or advantage therefrom; unless indeed they were compelled by penalty, which is in accord neither with economy or equal freedom.

To the second: It is probable that a discount of one-half of one per cent. per annum would meet the cost of such banking. But why should bankers, or their employees, be expected to work for bare support, while producers should have, when in excess of such support, the whole product of their labor, and so add to their capital the interest, not of the capital, but of their labor?

To the third: In the absence of State or collective meddling, competition would tend unquestionably to reduce discount to its lowest rate, which would ordinarily be something above cost. Otherwise at the vanishing point the banks also would disappear, though under the impulse of fierce competition they might sometimes discount, "sporadically," at cost, or even at a loss. The editor's words on economic rent seem appropriate here: "I believe that economic rent exists now, and would continue under freedom, but then with a tendency to decrease." Substitute interest for rent, and you have the case of economic interest, as distinguished from plutocratic interest.

Where land is embraced in the term capital, no casuistry can show a distinction between interest and rent; nor where interest is paid on mortgaged premises. The measure of both is the same. This measure, as given by economists, is highly misleading. Superior and inferior soils have very little to do with it. One man will starve on land of the same quantity and quality as those of the land from which another will obtain an increase over his support. Rent from urban and suburban places, and even much rural rent, has absolutely nothing whatever to do with the quality of land. In the latter case, it is largely owing to the necessity for restoring exhausted fertility and decaying premises. Increase is determined by facility for cooperation and the practical division of labor, by the degree of utility of novel appliances employed, and by wise adaption of capacity to special work. Bankers no more than laborers can rationally be expected to work without reasonable expectation of having their capital stock increased thereby. But, whatever the associated banks do for each other, it is illogical in the extreme to suppose that they will discount gratis the non-circulating credits of others with their well-established circulating credits. Those who have little credit or capital will be taxed, not according to cost of doing business, but according to their needs, under freedom as under law. Legal or combination rule may mitigate or aggravate, but cannot help their condition permanently. Their only escape is to cease borrowing.

It is quite true that without capital or credit the laborer might not be able to earn starvation wages; but it does not follow that therefore there must be some increase which arises from capital. And if such increase arises from capital, why not allow capital to have it? The editor must be aware that there is an obverse side to the capital and increase question. In a majority of cases the capital "comes home missing," or is not maintained intact. Failures are not especially experienced by those who start in their industrial career without capital, but rather by those who start with borrowed or inherited capital. Not capital, then, in kind or quality is the measure of interest, but the capacity and adaptability of the labor to it. Since the editor's principle premise is found to be erroneous, my contention is relieved of the several dilemmas in which the other five questions seek to involve it. The intrepid and ingenious worker, under freedom, will find or create the conditions and helps necessary to increase his wealth, or more desirable satisfaction, while the indolent or unwise one may only see his inherited or borrowed wealth disappear. Is it the capital or labor which has made or failed to make the increase? Surely, capital proves a most indeterminate factor as a self-creator.

I submit that, in distinguishing between economic interest and that which is the fruit of monopoly, the earning of the toiler from the plunder of the spoiler, I have invaded no right to use the old term without the qualifying phrase; I oppose that as strenuously as Liberty can. My idea explains many phenomena in wealth acquirement unexplainable by any extant theory, and is not to be accounted for as sporadic or epidemic. To me it appears the key which will open the doors of prosperity and happiness to the misguided and plundered toilers, who have but the sense and the courage to enter.

I should deeply regret the discontinuance of Liberty, or to see the doughty knight disheartened who has so long, and against fearful odds, upheld the hopeful standard, and helped me at advanced age to jump the ruts of absurd politico-economic superstitions. I should equally deplore seeing Liberty become authoritarian, or philosophical Anarchy a fossilized ism.

The power of the State or collectively to levy tribute, collect rack-rent, evict from land and home, enforce exhaustive usury, and aid plutocrats to plunder the increase labor has produced, is no non-essential, past, present, or future. The "common consent" to the exercise of these powers must be withdrawn ere we can have any salutary change in our industry, commerce, or finance. I trust that this assumption will not imperil Liberty or Anarchy. Let us have freedom, whether it will give us circulating credit without paying for its use or no. **J. K. INGALLS.**

Glenora, N. Y.

Intent upon my purpose of keeping the issue narrowed, I shall ignore for the present everything in the foregoing article except the answers to my three questions.

To my first question Mr. Ingalls answers that the bank of my hypothesis could issue its notes at a cost not exceeding its running expenses and incidental losses. So far, then, my claim is sustained.

But he answers further that such a bank could not exist in the absence of a motive for its existence. It remains for me, then, only to supply the motive. The task is easy. The thousand business men of my hypothesis would unite to form a bank of issue, and would connect this bank of issue with other similar banks for clearing purposes, because thereby they could establish a collective credit having circulating power, which each of them could obtain in exchange for his equally good but less reputable individual credit, having to pay therefor nothing but the cost of this exchange of credits. In other words, these business men would form such a bank as I describe in order to borrow money at less than one per cent. instead of paying, as they do now, from four to fifteen per cent. Is the motive sufficient?

To my second question Mr. Ingalls answers that the cost above referred to would probably be met by a discount of one-half of one per cent. Sustained again. I have not to discuss here why bank employees "should be expected to work for bare support." It suffices for the argument to know that what these employees are now willing to accept for their services can be paid to them out of funds pro-

vided by a discount of one-half of one per cent. And this Mr. Ingalls
admits. When we have exhausted the present issue, then I will
consider with him how many tears I can afford to shed over the sad
fate of those bank presidents for whom a discount of one-half of
one per cent. provides salaries of only ten, fifteen, and twenty thousand dollars. [I did not contemplate such salaries when I said one
half of one per cent. would probably pay the cost. Did he when he
put the question?]

The discussion now centres, therefore, upon the following question, which I put to Mr. Ingalls:

Is the desire to borrow money at less than one per cent., instead
of at four per cent. or more, a sufficient consideration to induce business men to form such banks as I have described?

If Mr. Ingalls answers that it is not, he must show why it is not.
If he answers that it is, then the proposition which, according to Mr.
Ingalls, has never been demonstrated, will have received its demonstration,—the proposition, namely, that free and mutual banking
will make it possible to procure capital without paying for its use
(the discount being charged, not for the use of capital, but to meet
expenses incidental to the transfer of capital).   T.

In March this communication and answer appeared.

THE INTEREST QUESTION NARROWED TO A POINT.

To the Editor of Liberty:

To your question: "Is the desire to borrow money at less than
one per cent. instead of more than four per cent. a sufficient consideration to induce business men to form such banks as I have described?" I answer: Yes! unquestionably, so far as the borrowers
are concerned.

Having thus released myself from the unilateral inquest, I will
add that, had you not excluded from the subject the lender, an equal
factor with the borrower and complementary to him, I could not
have made the answer you sought. Banks deal in "evidences of
debt." They sell as well as buy credits. Indeed, they "create them
out of nothing" to sell and exchange for other credits, and buy them
back to decreate into nothing again. Fiat credit is possible, not fiat
money. To obtain four or more per cent. interest is, therefore, an
inducement of equal strength with the one you describe, and can-

cels it. Interest at zero would leave the formation of your banks economically motiveless. Otherwise, they would have been formed long ago. Col. W. B. Green informed me forty-five years since that he was pressed by borrowers to form his mutual bank, but found no lenders, except a few philanthropists who would lend their money without interest anyway, and these he was unwilling to risk sacrificing in an untried experiment. The member who had more capital than he could use, and all that he could use, would be wholly indifferent to the rate, high or low, because he would get back in dividends all he paid out in discounts, less expense of the business, and no more. The members of all classes, contemplating lending to outsiders, would desire a high rate, and so turn the scale in favor of the high rate. '

The great Rochdale Association found it impracticable to sell their goods at cost, and so adopted the method of selling at the market price and dividing the profits among the members or adding to their capital. The mutual banks would find the same difficulty in selling their credits, and would doubtless adopt the same method of charging the current rate of interest, making dividends according to capital invested.

None but members could borrow 'at cost, or get their discounts returned in dividends.

What banking would be under industrial and commercial freedom can be foretold, I think, with some degree of certainty. What Anarchy would be under organized bank rule, mutualistic or otherwise, is as difficult to foresee as what government itself will become under our present plutocratic regime.

But what I have said I am not to be understood as affirming that some payments of interest may not be escaped, for they are now, and the costs as well, through forbearance of creditors, bankrupt acts, and other devices, honest or fraudulent. What I do mean is that in a general way interest is unescapable, like rent, profit, or taxes. The only question is whether comrades and governments shall enforce the economic or the monopolistic principle. While we have laws to enforce rent, interest, or profit-bearing contracts, other than as to the matters of equity, there is no safety for the debtor.

Whether your positions or mine have been sustained, or whether

we are mutually progressing on converging lines toward the point
where they coincide, can be of only personal interest. What the
readers of Liberty are interested in knowing is whether Anarchy is
to take along with it into the coming era rack-rent, evictions, mortgages, foreclosures, and the forces and methods of invasive power, in
defiance of the public good, the economics and Isonomics of social
science.   J. K. INGALLS.

Glenora, N. Y.

With apology to Mr. Ingalls for my persistence, I must continue
the "unilateral inquest" a little further, regretting that I have not
been relieved from doing so by an unequivocal answer to my last
question. The qualified answer that Mr. Ingalls gives is this: The
desire to borrow at less than one per cent. is a sufficient motive to
business men as borrowers to induce them to embark in mutual banking, but the desire to lend at more than four per cent. is a sufficient
motive to business men as lenders to keep them from embarking in
mutual banking. Now I must ask for answers to the following questions:

(1) Does the business man who has capital but lacks cash—that is,
the business man who wishes to borrow—sacrifice, by engaging with
others in mutual banking, any opportunity of lending (at four per
cent. or any other rate) which he enjoys before so engaging?

(2) If so, what?

(3) If not; if the business man in question, by embarking with
others in mutual banking, does not thereby damage himself as lender,—is not the desire to borrow at less than one per cent. a sufficient consideration to induce him to so embark?

I respectfully insist on answers to these questions. Mr. Ingalls is a
very able and sincere writer on economic problems. He deservedly
exercises an influence on the class of people to whom Liberty appeals.
Repeatedly during its publication he has come forward with a denial
of the position that mutual banking will make it possible to borrow
money without interest. I have now determined to force him, once
and for all, to make good this denial by proof, or else to retract it.
Only by refusing to answer me can he avoid a choice between these
two courses; and, as he is an eminently frank and honest man, he
will not refuse to answer me. When he has acknowledged his error,

or by his answers has forced me to acknowledge mine, I will discuss with him the other points which he raises, and especially the extraordinary statement which he attributes to Colonel Greene.   T.

In May the conclusion:

POINT OF THE INTEREST QUESTION.

To the Editor of Liberty:

Before replying to your questions as amended, but still so ambiguous as to invite equivocal answers, I will briefly attempt to ascertain where we are (at) in this discussion. At the conclusion of my brief essay on "Unescapable Interest" I had invited discussion of the truth of what was new in it. I confess to surprise that, "instead of a book' or even a paragraph of argument, I was met by a string of questions, with claim of a right to force answers, and refusal to discuss the question until there were no question to discuss and until I should retract or refuse to retract a denial I had never made,—viz., that "mutual banking will make it possible to borrow money without interest"; or that a free market will have a tendency to reduce the rate of interest to an equilibrium, zero. It does not seem to have occurred to the editor that a "free market" embraced anything more than liberty to divide, coin, and circulate credits and commodities, or that freedom to produce, possess, and exchange wealth were necessary before free banking could have more than a theoretical existence.

To your early question I answered that it was based on three conditions, neither of which was even supposable without a desire to derive some advantage, profit, or interest therefrom. In the editor's eagerness to make me "'fess," he did not become aware that, in establishing the existence of a motive for mutual banking, he at the same time established the existence of economic rent or interest for the use of capital, since the reduction of the percentage would be so much gained to capital or to the increased profit of labor in the use of capital. His contention that the use of capital increases production is an admission of the same kind.

In order to avoid misuse of terms, I think we should use the word usury for monopoly interest, which is its exact meaning, while interest proper should be called interest still, as that is its original meaning,—"premium for the use of capital" being only one, and the fifth in order, of Webster's definitions. It might also be used to indicate that portion of interest after it has been captured from the rightful holder; but usury is a better term for that. Rent, which is synonymous with interest or usury, is also used to denote the normal advantage of superior soil or location, whether held by the occupier or captured by a landlord; and rent from use of more or better capital, whether enjoyed by user, or plundered by lord of money or capital, is still called rent, as in France, or annuity, as in England.

The discussion seems to have arrived at a point capable or reduction to a syllogism something like this: Interest, or increase of labor's production from use of capital, or saving of the same, is the efficient motive for forming mutual banks; but mutual banks will kill interest; therefore, mutual banks will kill the motive for their formation.

A deduction less absurd would be; the interest constituting the motive to form mutual banks is a wholly different thing, or a different relation of the same thing, from the thing the banks were formed to kill. But this deduction would give the case to economic rent, interest, etc.

I can now proceed to answer the questions last propounded, in which the ambiguity still lingers. "Business men" are not all borrowers, unless they are all lenders as well. The first question relates to borrowers only. I should say that a borrowing business man would lose no opportunity he ever had to lend at any rate of interest, because to be able to lend would make him a lending business man, to whom the question does not refer; but to be able to borrow at one per cent. might increase his opportunity greatly (as a lender). For example the national banks, who borrow at one per cent., or less, of government (yet do not lend at a less rate on that account.)

The second question is made unnecessary by the answer to the first. The third requires also an alternative. The borrowing business man would have a reasonable consideration for forming a mutual bank; a lending business man would have none. National Bankers, with little cash and considerable capital (bonds), are induced to form national banks; but there are many private banks and State banks who have more cash than capital, who do not avail themselves of the opportunity, and many national banks have thrown up their charters and gone again to private or State banking, some of whom are now paying their depositors three per cent. on their deposits, and even six per cent.

I shall be ready to recant my heresy whenever it is shown that the "saving grace" of mutual banking for discount purposes, and the capitalization of debts, is a cardinal doctrine of the Anarchistic church; but I think the editor will first retract his endorsement of economic rent, or else his denial of the existence of economic interest, unless he is able to compromise on the "sporadic" in both. I am centrain he will be unable to show wherein rent and interest differ; which I would be glad to have him attempt. It would also greatly gratify me to have him explain the nature of the "appropriate legislation" by which he will prohibit the ignorant and shiftless worker from exchanging a part of his natural wages (the increase) with a boss, dealer, pawn-broker, or lender who will relieve him from a little care, exertion, or responsibility, or discount the fruits of his toil before ripening, and on such terms as the two may agree upon. [That would consist with despotism not freedom]. I think the editor mistakes greatly the character of the labor dollar of Andrews, the labor note of Warren, and particularly the labor check of the Labor Exchange. The purpose is not, as I understand, to create a bank of discount, or a loan association, but to employ an instrument or tool, to effect a ready completion of commodity exchanges, in order to counteract the evil to commerce of our present financial credits, which operate to aid the forestaller to hold commodities out of market for a rise, resulting in periodical gluts, financial panics, and industrial crises.

Lending has not the remotest relation to exchange. I can understand that completion of one side to an exchange can be deferred and usury charged up as a penalty therefor. But how a loan can become an exchange without compounding the penalty—in itself a misdemeanor—I do not see, or how it can even then become a factor in exchange. Credit other than the strictly commercial adds in no way to the circulation of commodities, to the amount of land, or to the capacity to labor. Credit and money are economic factors only as they become instruments in facilitating the completion of exchanges, [not when deferring it].

It becomes necessary, first, to show an economic necessity for borrowing, which at the same time will prove the impossibility of killing interest, either economic or monopolistic. Indebtedness and

usury are inseparable, except through repudiation or a bankrupt
law. Now, if a necessity exists for borrowing, or if there be even
an unreasoning demand for loans, the same remuneration, including increase, will be commanded by the lender as that which is
received in other lines of business. If no such necessity exists, there
can be no necessity for banks of discount. If lending be a benefit
to the borrower, or compatible with the public weal, which I in general terms deny, it cannot be had without paying its market price.
If it is not a benefit, but, as a rule, an injury, there is no call for
interference to enforce its agreements.

I trust the editor has exaggerated his position by intimating that
he has no use for Liberty, unless it will enable mutual banks to
abolish interest. It is no exaggeration to say that the correspon-
dent has no occasion for an anarchy which is to become the
instrument of invasive barbarisms, bonds, mortgages, fore-closures,
evictions, forfeitures of land, home, opportunity to labor, and even
of personal freedom. The enslaving "sacred contract" has no attraction for me. "The light it sheds saves not, but damns, the
world."

If my answers suit the editor, and he feels sustained in his positions, and that he has demonstrated theoretically what I declared
had never been demonstrated positively, my general positions still
remain unquestioned and unquestionable,—viz:

First, that from labor, through use of land and capital, all increment, economic interest, is derived.

Second, that all hiring of land, of capital (or of money, if you
will), under monopoly, is tribute extracted from the interest earned
by labor.

Third, that such tribute under such dependence is inevitable while
the monopolies are legally sustained.

And I will add a fourth by way of suggestion: The abolition of
land rent would greatly reduce the tribute now exacted by all other
monopolies. Abolition of other rents could not in any way reduce
tribute from the use of land or ownership of labor, but would rather
tend to increase them.   J. K. INGALLS,

Glenora, N. Y.

THE VANISHING POINT REACHED.

Mr. J. K. Ingalls seems to imagine that the answers which he now gives to my last series of questions are as equivocal as his answer to my previous question. Not so. The terms in which he answered my previous question implied two opposite motives influencing at the same time a business man fulfilling a double capacity,—as borrower and lender,—and cancelling each other. As my question did not concern men who, as individuals, were in the market as lenders, but only those who were in the market as borrowers, this answer was equivocal. But the answers now given to my last question distinctly recognized the borrowing business man and the lending business man as two individuals, and this recognition removes all the equivocation; for the desire of a lender to lend at a high rate cannot cancel the desire of a borrower to borrow at a low rate, provided the borrower, by association with other borrowers, can provide himself with a source from which to borrow at a low rate,—a condition not as paradoxical as it seems, since the fact of association creates a credit that before had no existence.

The present answers, then, being straight-forward and satisfactory, let us review the admissions which I have secured. Mr. Ingalls has admitted that business men desiring to borrow have an adequate motive for embarking in mutual banking (see his article in the present issue); he has admitted that the loans of a mutual bank's credit would cost the bank nothing but running expenses and incidental outlays and losses (see No. 305); he has admitted that this cost would probably be covered by a discount of one-half of one per cent. (see No. 305); and he has admitted that, "in the absence of State or collective meddling, competition would tend unquestionably to reduce discount to its lowest term, which would ordinarily be something above cost" (see No. 305). I have interpreted this last admission as meaning that in banking the force of competition would have a tendency of the same strength as that which it has in other businesses similarly free from physical limitations,—in other words, that the tendency would be strong enough to cause the price to hover around the cost limit, now rising a little above it, now falling a little below it, but averaging cost, or perhaps a shade more. In neither of the two articles which Mr. Ingalls has written since this interpretation appeared has he taken any exception to it. I am justified therefore in assuming that he admits this also.

Now, this series of admissions constitutes the entire case for mutual banking. Whether or not it was ever demonstrated before that mutual banking would abolish the payment of interest for the use of borrowed money, I have now led Mr. Ingalls to demonstrate this himself. His declarations show that under freedom the rate of discount would fall to nearly one-half of one per cent. This is equivalent to the abolition of the payment of interest, for in such a money market an individual case of interest payment would cut no figure economically, any more than one's occasional payment of a quarter to an urchin for delivering a letter cuts a figure now that letter-postage has fallen to two cents. Mr. Ingalls has formally allowed that mutual banking will do all that it claims for itself, and he is forever debarred from repeating that denial or doubt of its claims which has been heard from him at intervals for many years. I began this little campaign of question and answer for the purpose of silencing this gun, and I have effectually done it.

Thus ends this matter. Now Mr. Ingalls desires me to discuss with him the question of the existence of what he calls economic interest,—that is, the question whether people can do more with capital than without it. He asks me to retract my "denial of the existence of economic interest." I pledge him my word that I will retract it as soon as he shall quote to me the passage in which the denial occurred. There exists no such passage. To have denied so trite a truth would have been no less remarkable than Mr. Ingalls's grave persistence in affirming it. I do not approve the new use that Mr. Ingalls makes of the word interest, but I have nothing to say in dispute of the entirely undisputed idea which he expresses by the phrase "economic interest." When he denied my position, I had a right to expect him to answer my questions. When he shall show that I have denied his position, he will have a similar right to expect me to answer his questions. And, if he drives me into a corner, I swear that he shall hear no complaint from me that he is trying to "force answers."

But, while I have as yet no occasion to discuss "economic interest" with Mr. Ingalls, it is fitting that I should answer him on certain incidental points that he has made concerning the manner in which mutual banking may be put into practice, and with these matters I purpose to deal in a later article.   T.

CHAPTER XVII.

A carefull review of the discussion in the previous chapter, will I think enable the reader to discover that it was carried on under mutual misapprehension. Mr. Tucker conceived that Mr. Ingalls denied that freedom in banking would make possible the procuring of capital without paying for its use; when Mr. Ingalls had only asserted that no banking device could wholly "eradicate interest," "kill interest," altogether. The latter had imagined that Mr. Tucker had denied that "economic interest" existed at all, when he had only said that it would "disappear as an economic factor," and could have nothing but a "sporadic" life under a conceivable system of Mutual Banking.

Hence the debate on parallel lines without satisfaction to either. The issue turned really upon the third question, as no difference arose on the other two, although Mr. T. claimed their admission as distinctly sustaining his position. Mr. I. not being a metaphysician or "master of logic," like his opponent, was slow to apprehend the little game, which had been put up on him; "this little campaign of question and answer for the purpose of silencing this gun," which had been annoying Mr. T. so long. That he may "have effectually done it " must be so, for he is "an able and sincere writer." To my lay mind however, a deduction from a hypothetical premise, acknowledged to be "paradoxical," falls far short of being a scientific demonstration. That he is right, is still probable, since mutual friends think with him; notably comrades Henry Cohen who avers we cannot avoid going in debt, but can avoid paying interest on it; A. L. Ballou, Geo. H. Coursen, Jr., Francis D. Tandy, author of Voluntary Socialism and Joseph A. Labadie. The latter was called to account, by the way, for writing so loosely as to allow "J. K. Ingalls and others to put nonsense into his words." Mr. Tandy has not yet been brought to book, although he gives away the mutual bank hypothesis, by assuming that banking will become under equal freedom, mainly an individual affair.

But there can be no doubt as to the silence of the gun, so far as the columns of Liberty are concerned. My name has not appeared in its columns, but once for two years, and that only to designate as "nonsense," a little notice I sent it commending Labadies' lecture at Detroit, one word of which, it was not allowed the readers of Liberty to see.

After the great triumph in his "campaign of questions," had ended "this matter," he promised to answer me, "on certain incidental points," of the facts and science of banking, at a later day. This was repeated once or more in the course of the debate and by letter and also personally to me; yet a prudent silence has remained unbroken, even as to "the extraordinary statement" attributed by me to Col. Green. But there were other mediums through which my pen was able to reach some of Liberty's readers. When Westrup's book appeared I wrote a lengthy criticism upon it, exposing its fallacy in placing the money question before the land question; the impossibility of making "the abolition of usury unavoidable," and showing that while denouncing the idea of a standard of value as a gross absurdity, he had, in successive sections, proved that labor furnished both such measure and standard.

When Cohen's edition of Greene's Mutual Banking was issued, I was requested as a member of the A. W. Corps, to write a notice of it. I did, and sent it to Mr. Cohen. He returned it saying he could not use it, as he did not agree with me on the subject of debt; that debt was the order of the day, and any banking system must provide for it.

When Mr. Tandy's book appeared, I wrote a notice commending the general scope and treatment of the subject, but pointing out an error or two where he had followed Tucker and Bilgram in regard to failure to perform contracts, who claimed it was an invasion and to be punished as crime, and showing that while he had appeared to favor the Mutual Bank fad, had actually given it away.

These were all brought to Mr. Tucker's attention; he has ignored them all, as he had a perfect right to do; but which I feel certain he would not have done, if he had thought he could have answered them satisfactorily, or worked another little campaign of questions. Still much consideration should be shown him for his over tasked hours, in his endeavors to keep Liberty afloat, and to promote the great principle for which it stands, and to which his hobby is not a very serious obstacle.

That economic rent will continue under Freedom as under conventional statutes, a positive factor, there seems no doubt. That it will also prove, and perhaps as often, a negative one does not invalidate the position, but strengthens it. Mr. T. does not think it probable that economic rent will wholly disappear. Nor is it more probable that economic interest will do so.

Say the economists, "who so holds land of a better quality than such as would be worked without rent, holds rent, and the only question is whether he shall enjoy it himself or sell it to another." It is the same with capital. That legal money more readily commands interest than commodities, is because it is a lien on every kind of property and commands that especial commodity, which is best fitted to the requirements of the user, and to his ability to use. Mr. Tucker recognizes the tendency of rent to disappear, yet admits it improbable that it will ever do so wholly. But when I show that interest is not likely to wholly disappear for the same reason, he assumes that his ingenious, not ingenuous questioning, has compelled me to demonstrate that my contention was disproved.

With his contention, tendency to disappear, means possible but not probable disappearance. With mine it always means positive disappearance; and nothing else!

The only noticeable point of difference between us is, as to whether monopoly of land or of money is the greater evil. But this difference is more in the statement than in the substance. Whether there is a greater robbery through the ground rent, or through the rent of money and capital in buildings and plant, there can be no question; but whether the ground rent is the fundamental rent, on which the other depends, or is, as Kellogg contended, dependent on the interest rate, is another question. Assuming the disappearance or great reduction of interest on money and capital, through the repeal of unequal legislation about money and capital, while unlimited owner-ship, or dominion of land remained, it would not have the slightest effect on the amounts of ground rent collected. It would enormously increase the price of land; out a farm rented on the Metayer System and yielding to the owner 500 bushels of grain, or its equivalent, would still rent for the same.

The fatal fallacy in the case as held by Mr. Tucker is, the ignoring of the voluntary borrowing and paying of interest on the part of many persons in business and out of business, where "an inducement is given to the endorser of a note," and as a bonus, where the importunate spendthrift, who desires immediate means, and the gambler with money, stocks or speculative enterprise, who can, or thinks he can increase his chances by the use of large funds, eagerly accepts any terms to obtain the means to follow his bent or fancy.

Were all men judicious, free from vice and error or hallucinations of any kind, a possibility of the disappearance of interest, might be argued with some plausibility. There seems but one possibility of stopping interest; that of stopping borrowing, and that one not a thing probable ever to occur. There is no need however that laws should compel its payment, since borrowing is not business, but a weakness and subject to ethical not economic consideration. A contract is either equitable or inequitable in itself, without reference to the conditions and restrictions under which it is made. If not so it would be impossible to judge whether the restrictions were baneful or salutary. The organized invasion consists in enforcing an unjust contract, whether made under freedom or under duress, for although the existence of duress vitiates the contract, it proves nothing but a presumption as to its justice.

Would I then deny Freedom of contract to borrower and lender? Certainly not. But I do deny most emphatically that by such contract they can rightfully bind me, or any other member of the body politic, to the obligation of coercing the fulfillment of an argeement, which is in itself inequitable. Our Courts of Law no longer hold valid contracts to render service. The single exception of Seamen's indentures is being contested, and both the justice and utility of their enforcement is being questioned.

That mutual banks would benefit anybody but members is greatly problematical; that they would not do so except indirectly is admitted by their advocates. With the great number of mutual insurance companies in our country, the rates of insurance have increased instead of diminished, and the multiplication of mutual banks, might have no better effect on the discounting of notes, except to those able to discount their own through the combination. Those needing discount the most, in most need of borrowing, would still have to go to the state or private bank and stand the shave. To take from the state however the power to enforce usurious contracts, would make the payment of interest voluntary, and prove the only means of avoiding the enforcement of injustice.

A year or more before the appearance of the first article in this controversy, an article was sent to Liberty and printed with comments by Mr. Tucker, which shows the narrow margin open to discussion but which he made the most of. It was as follows:

INTEREST JUST AND UNJUST.

In the address of Mr. Hugo Bilgram (Liberty of April 22) is found much to approve. What he says about the interest on privileged money can be questioned by no honest criticism. It is simply unjust. Whether there is not interest of another kind, and other sources which produce monopolistic interest, are quite other questions. To me it seems plain that there are economic conditions which produce interest independent of monopoly, and that there are several monopolies, besides that of money, which bear an unjust interest.

Patent right, government privilege to follow certain productive callings and to buy and sell goods, are joint factors with privileged money in yielding onerous interest. And beneath all these lies the legal protection to unlimited dominion of the land. Whether "the government prescribes the number of shoes in the country," or prescribes the number of shoemakers, the people will have to pay the interest or profit, and suffer the inconvenience, caused by unjust legislation, the same as when compelled to hire money from a privileged banker. It is far worse when the government yields up to the control of the class who are able to buy into it, the dominion of all the fruit-yielding land to the exclusion of the people, who have now to hire the natural sources of all wealth.

Nor do I quite agree with him that the interest-bearing power of money confers the profit-bearing power upon capital. On the contrary, I am quite sure that capital, particularly land, could not be bought at all with money which bore no interest, because, in the absence of all money, monopolized land would be let to the laborer, as has been done in all time, without valuation in the terms of money at all, for a part of the annual produce of the labor applied. I doubt not that interest would continue, if lawful money was abolished and the circulation of credits left free. If one owns a farm from which he cannot raise more than a bare subsistence, he can pay no interest to mortgagee or banker. No one hires money for its own sake. All know it to be barren. So far as a direct exchange is concerned, it matters not whether money be cheap or dear. The simultaneous exchanges will be affected in the same way. The terms in money make no difference to the relative values of the things exchanged. It is only when one wants to buy and has nothing to buy with that he needs to borrow money. It is not the producer as such, but only the borrower, who suffers wrong. It is only the lender who is benefited.

But there is a variable rate of interest, profit, or rent, arising from the use of capital, not at all attributable to legal monopolies of any kind, but which capitalism has succeeded by the aid of "appropriate legislation" in engrossing. It is the whole product of labor, save a bare support to the laborer, or, what is nearly the same thing, the difference between what he would produce co-operating with the capital, or by working without it. This is more particularly true of the land, without which labor can pay no interest on money legal or free, or indeed effect any product whatever. Hence unconditioned dominion of the land is the ultimate source of all tributary interest, rent, or profits, the three being different only in name.

Besides the tributary increment, the same thing appears under economic law, released from the State class laws, and which arises from the ability of labor to produce more than it consumes, and which normally, under equal freedom, becomes the property of the laborer, and is therefore not inequitable or unjust, because promotive of the general industrial prosperity.   J. K. INGALLS.

A NEW CONCEPTION OF INTEREST.

The article on interest by J. K. Ingalls, printed in another column, does not seem to me to be written in its author's usual clear style. Some of his positions are true without qualification, but others can be regarded as true only by using the word interest in an entirely new sense.

If rent and profit are to be considered interest, then it is true that "there are several monopolies, besides that of money, which bear an unjust interest"; I presume that this would be readily admitted by Mr. Bilgram, whom Mr. Ingalls is criticising. This, however, is not a very serious departure from economic terminology.

More violent is the use of the word interest to express the entire extra product resulting from labor's use of capital. If I, who can produce only ten without a spade, succeed in producing twenty with a borrowed spade, for the use of which I pay six, then in Mr. Ingalls's view, if I understand him, the interest on the spade includes not only the six paid for its use, but the entire extra ten produced by its use. This is intelligible, but to me it is novel. So defining interest, one finds no difficulty in granting, again, that "there are economic conditions which produce interest indepedent of monopoly." And since Mr. Ingalls appears to admit that under equal freedom the entire extra ten would fall to me as laborer, and that six would no longer go to the owner of the spade, I am not at all disposed to dispute the justice of interest so defined, and, far from desiring to abolish it. hope to see it vastly multiplied.

But I wonder if Mr. Ingalls uses the word in this sense when he says that "capital, particularly land, could not be bought at all with money which bore no interest." If so, then still again can I understand and agree with him. For in this sense money that bears no interest means simply money that does not contribute to labor's power of production and such money is necessarily representative of no property whatsoever, has no power to circulate, and will not be taken in exchange for anything of value. But thus interpreted the statement is so insignificant that Mr. Ingalls must, it seems to me, have used the word in its usual sense. In that case, however, insignificance is simply replaced by absurdity. For what can be more absurd than to say that a non-interest-bearing note, based upon specific property and for the redemption of which said property can be legally seized, will not be taken in exchange for other property approximating in value that of the property serving as security for the note? It is indeed conceivable that, if the money monopoly were abolished and land monopoly remained, land would rise in value; but it cannot be held for a moment, with any show of reason, that it would bear no price.   T.

I am sure the reader will congratulate me on the favorable criticism of an article written really in my usual obscure style; for he makes my meaning not only very plain; but readily admits it, for himself and Mr. Bilgram, as a not "very serious departure from economic terminology." Although he thinks my use of the word interest more violent, by an illustration shows it to be not only intelligible but "novel." He is "not at all disposed to dispute the justice of interest so defined," but wonders if I use the word in the same sense, in a statement with a trifling bearing on the main question, as to whether non-interest-bearing money would buy rent bearing land. Now since money is a mere counter or tally of commodity values, and which values as of land and productive plant, are based upon the increase they will yield, a money commanding only property without increase could not possibly purchase property bearing increase. His illustration is not to the point. "A non-interest bearing note based upon specific property," which is subject to seizure through governmental aid in case of default, is not a money of redemption, is merely a certificate of a deposit of specific property, which requires no bank of any kind to make but only a warehouse. A money which accrues no interest corresponding to rent of land and to the increase from capital in the different employments in which business men are engaged, is not representative, and could not circulate as a medium of exchange.

If Mr. Tucker's property upon which his non-interest bearing note is based, is property bearing rent or interest on profit above cost of service, on what principle of equity or simple economy can he refuse to render such rent interest or profit, or a portion thereof to the holder of the note, by use of which he has been enabled to appropriate such increase to himself.' If such "specific property should chance to be Mr. T.'s home, working tools, necessary plant to effect his annual production, I think he can have no clear apprehension of what that involves; mortgage of home and opportunity to work. A mortgage is simply an instrument to legalize invasion: and was once what its name still signifies, a death-gage or pledge, following from the gage of battle, in which the vanquished was saved from death on condition of yielding himself a slave to the victor, with power of life and death over him. The "sacredness" of the contract secured unquestioning obedience to all the master's commands, and whose power was thus perpetuated. At once it became an instrument also of reducing freemen to bondage, allowing no defense to invasion, and more effectual than the sword. Death was the penalty for failure to discharge a debt, at the option of the creditor.

And it is difficult to see how it is possible to coerce the payment of debt without involving the loss of home, liberty and even life. To take away one's environment and possessions involves all this. If one refuses to pay, redress can only be obtained by seizing his person and compelling his labor, which potentially reduces him to slavery and holds his life at hazard.

We should consider the distinction between the money of commerce, and the money devised by governments to effect the enslavement of labor. Such money is wholly different from the money of exchange, as it tends to obstruct rather than promote exchange. Lending and borrowing has no relation to commerce in any way. Commerce deals with exchange of commodities, not pledges nor forfeitures. Banks for hoarding and lending, deal in "evidences of debt," not commodities, and have no economic significance. They in no wise promote completion of the art of exchanging wealth or advance production but retard both. No equation can be made with usury, unless it be as a penalty for deferring completion of an exchange, or a charge for services. If the latter, the borrower can have no reasonable complaint against paying its price.

Mortgages of land and homes, mean all the term implies; forfeiture of land, of home, of happiness, of liberty, of life. Anarchy cannot hinder knaves and fools from entering into such contracts, farther than to refuse to enfore them and so decline to contribute to the "reversion to type," brutal and barbaric, which now threatens our civilization.

There can be no justification for enforcing contracts of indebtedness other than upon the ground that such use of force would tend to reduce the repudiation of such indebtedness arising from misfortune or fraudulent purpose. Enforcement can be effected only by enslaving the debtor. "The borrower is slave to the lender" is axiomatic, as verified by the unvarying testimony of history. Borrowing and lending is not only hazardous to both parties, like the primitive gage of battle, but a public calamity. Leaving the creditor without legal redress will reduce borrowing to a minimum. The lender acts under no duress, and acts voluntarily, and should not have power to put or keep the borrower in duress. This would vastly increase the stability of the commercial credit, which is simply a confidence that a purchaser will complete the exchange; and so make fraudulent and "plunger" transactions nearly impossible. Personal liberty and public prosperity both require that all enforcement and invasion should be abandoned, and the whole matter be placed beyond the control of government, or even of the inconsiderate impulse of anarchistic juries.

When it is understood by the lender, that he cannot fall back upon the law or comrades to enforce payment, borrowing is no invasion of equal freedom, though annoying solicitation might become invasive. Reduction of the rate of interest, would afford only temporary relief even to the borrower in financial trouble, since the chronic borrower would only be encouraged by it to take a deeper plunge. The great mass of bankruptcies are of those who have borrowed at low rates, as well as those who have borrowed at extra high rates, and includes those who through favor or forbearance, pay no interest at all. The fraud and dead beat does not hesitate to offer impossible rates. In the hundreds—thousands, I have lent without interest in the last 40 years, I do not call to mind but one borrower, who was in the least benefitted thereby. The only time I was ever benefitted by borrowing, was when I was paying 8 per cent on a considerable sum.

The utter folly of enforcing lender's and borrower's contracts, is seen in the attempts to remedy the mischief they have done in deranging business and enslaving labor by more law—stay law, bankrupt law, exemption laws and laws of limitation, by last of which, if on a "book account" payment is deferred 6 years, not only the penalty for delay but the debt itself is cancelled. Even a written contract under all "the solemnity of a seal" is set aside if by neglect payment is successfully deferred for 20 years.

To trust out goods at all is the reverse of an economic act—a business vice. To put capital into the hands of a man incapable of administering it is to subvert its economic use, and to injure not benefit the recipient. The competent user of capital has little difficulty in obtaining it. It is more difficult for capital to find a judicious operator. From the debt side of the financial situation, disasters, defalcations and bankruptcies mainly proceed.

It is such points as these Mr. Tucker proposes to discuss with me later. I am a patient man, and soon he can possibly have opportunity to discuss the issues by himself. At eighty-one I can hardly expect to have a two or three year's term many times repeated.

CHAPTER XVIII.

In quite early youth, the ethics of the sex relations were presented to my mind. All matters of this kind were studiously tabooed or mystified, and therefore more attractive to my untutored imagination. Sometimes indifferently exact information would be communicated by vulgar men, and elder companions already misled by excited fancies and prurient curiosity.

A most sad occurence to a near neighbor of ours, a young man who had visited the city and returned home to die from a nameless disease so shocked me that when I went there to live, solicitation from lewd women had no temptation for me. I was not so safe however from the corrupting influence of my own sex. And I shall never cease to remember with gratitude the salutary influence derived from the lectures of Sylvester Graham, given to young men on sexual abuse.

From the present standpoint of later investigations, I suppose his science is now hardly considered up to date; but he was a pioneer in this work and made possible the simplification of physiology, and its special application to matters before veiled in mystery to the common mind. The misfortune of a neighbor's daughter to have a child without a husband, and the obloquy heaped upon mother and child by otherwise kindly disposed persons, excited my childish wonder. The mother's after life was orderly and exemplory and the daughter was beautiful and amiable, and they became in time restored to the respect and confidence of the same people who had at first scorned and ostracised them.

After my removal to New York, I became acquainted with Thomas L. and Mary Gove Nichols, Stephen Pearl Andrews, Albert Brisbane Henry Clapp and others, who affected great lattitude in the "freedom of the affections." I saw them at reform, association and spiritualist meetings, and favoring free speech on all questions of human interest, met them without serious prejudice. I was however so much engrossed with the subject of the Land, that I was seldom drawn to their special gatherings. But for the interest these persons took in industrial and economic questions, they would probably have had no reference here. Mr. Andrews as an Individualist excited my admiration for the able analysis of the social relations, and his remarkable cleverness of statement of the economic and financial problems. Mr. Brisbane was a Fourierite, and more of a collectivist; but he also held pronounced opinions on the land and labor questions, and both he and Mr. Andrews in a general way endorsed my utterances on these subjects whenever we met as we often did on many different platforms. This was particularly so in the Liberal Club, as long as I continued a member. In the Liberal Club I also met Mr. Bouchet, Mr. Ormsbey, Dr. Van Der Weyde, Dr. Lambert, and a number of others whose critcism favorable, unfavorable or severe were of great benefit to me in the way of suggestion, enabling me to supply omissions and correct my own mistakes. I should apologize perhaps to Mr. Samuel Leavitt, for not mentioning his name before. But he has been met on so many different platforms, I scarce know where to place him, particularly. We were in accord on the land and interest problems; but differed politically on the tariff and the greenback questions, although I acted as treasurer for the Liberty Bell, which he published in the Peter Cooper Presidential campaign. He advocated rational divorce for mismated couples. He has been a newspaper man ever since I knew him. He was the author of "Caliban and Shylock," "Peace Maker Grange," a social romance, and "Our Money War," a most elaborate and exact statement of the history of our money metallic or paper, since the existence of our nation, with a bias in favor of fiat money.

I should also mention Mrs. Elizabeth Cady Stanton, Susan B. Anthony and Mrs. Lillie Deveran Blake, Victoria Woodhull and others, identified with Woman Suffrage, who also manifested an interest in questions purely industrial and economical.

Soon after the close of the war, Miss Anthony, Mrs. Stanton with Parker Pillsbury as editor, commenced the publication of "The Revolution," a radical paper advocating mainly Woman Suffrage, but admitting papers in other subjects. I commenced a series of articles on money and finance which were received in a friendly spirit and published. At Miss Anthony's invitation, I addressed a meeting of the working girls' association in Elizabeth street, on economics as they affected the legal status of Woman, and on the injustice of laws, which discriminates against one half of mankind. Mrs. Stanton particularly has taken advanced ground on the labor, land and other subjects of economic significance. I have not felt called upon to note any recollections of the woman's rights agitation, since it is a political rather than an industrial and social one; but from early youth, when my mother insisted on a voice in school meetings and the Misses Thompsons of Sekonk, refused to pay taxes, because they were not allowed to vote, I have never had any doubt as to the equality of rights of the sexes. I have since changed my ideas as to the justice of voting for either man or woman; doubting the wisdom of determining questions of rights and duties by a show of hands, or a game of ballot box stuffing. And there are more ways than one to play it. Even could a majority of all be honestly obtained, why should their will be given domination over the minority to tax them without their consent, and enforce protection which they do not desire!

I often met Mrs. Blake at Peace meetings, and also at other reform meetings. She ever expressed much interest in economic subjects, though always giving precedence to the suffrage question.

With Mrs. Woodhull I became acquainted at meetings of the International Working Men's Association. She organized a section which met in her parlors, in west Twenty-eighth street, I think. She was an enthusiast in the doctrines they promulgated, and displayed a wonderful insight into economic and social subjects. At first it was thought that she merely echoed the thoughts of some of the radical minds which surrounded her, but her later contributions to Social and humanitary literature leaves little doubt that the brilliant address in 1872 before the New England Labor League and her later masterly presentation of the Social Problem at the Academy of Music were the product of her own finely organized brain.

After eighteen years of married life with her talented and genial English husband, whom in widowhood she now mourns, there should be no occasion to refer to the early discussion of the proprieties of her advocacy of mooted social theories. She has published for five years "The Humanitarian," a magazine of great merit on all the lines the name indicates.

Having necessarily referred to a number of persons friends of reform in labor and economic relations who have advocated also greater freedom in the marriage relation, and the wisdom of divorces in cases where great hardship or incompartibility existed. I hope I may be pardoned for digressing somewhat from the lines of pure reminiscence to discuss the question of the sex relationship at least in so far as to inquire what is the direction to which the present agitation is tending!

With my present views of government, there would only be courts of equity, as to matters of personal interests and relations. No laws of master and slave, of landlord and tenant, of creditor and debtor of husband and wife, of superior and inferior; but only of persons. equal before the tribunal. And with real jury trials where ever penalties or damages were involved; the law as well as fact being submitted to their judgments, and equal freedom and equal justice to constitute the standard, by which all decisions should be tested.

In 1853 the Spiritualists held meetings in Dodsworth Hall. The first lease was taken in my name. Lectures were continued there for many years. T. L. Harris, S. B. Brittan, Dr. and Mrs. Hallock, Judge Edmonds, and many other popular speakers were employed. Mrs.

Emma Hardinge Britton, Louise Kellogg, and her mother and father sang and played for them. There were also conferencs, where short speeches were made and discussions took place. I often spoke in these, but usually insisted that we should apply our spirituality in equalizing conditions and compensations here, and give the human spirit opportunity of harmonious development in this life.

There occasionally arose the question as to how far "free love" might be discussed. Judge Edmonds was for keeping the respectability of our undertaking untarnished, and reminded us that "order is Heaven's first law." To which it was replied that Heaven was abundantly able to take care of its laws and that to restrict freedom of investigation "might happly find us fighting against God."

It was remarked by some that those most intolerant of free discussion, had characters for chastity which would suffer most by close investigation. The advocates of the broader social freedom were evidently honest and while unguarded and even fanatical in expression, led no double life.

In 1853 an organization was formed and held sociables in Taylor's Hotel Hall, 555 Broadway. I attended many of their early meetings. There was speaking, music, singing and dancing. I spoke there several times upon economic and agrarian themes. The speeches were sometimes broad, but never indecent or vulgar. The conduct was orderly and respectful, and I saw no actions surpassing the improprieties of the kissing and romping games, I have often witnessed at Sectarian sociables, where dancing and cards were religiously prohibited.

During that summer, many of the wives and daughters of members were absent from the city on usual vacation. Partners for the men who remained were scarce. To remedy this a plan was devised which proved disastrous in the end. It was to charge single men not only the same admission fee as for a couple, but double the price. While this considerably reduced the number of single tickets sold, it reduced also the disparity between the numbers of the respective sexes. But such men as were attracted merely to the dance, and were vexed at the double charge, began to invite any woman they could induce to go without reference to character. Some even went to the street and picked up a companion from the demi-monde. Recognizing the women of the street, the police thought they were going to a house of assignation, and supposed they had discovered a place where they could levy blackmail, or gain some cheap notoriety by posing as guardians of the public morals. Accordingly the place was raided. A few were arrested, though nothing improper was found or reported. But the action effectually broke up the association.

Through some business transaction in fruit, I became acquainted with some members of the Oneida Community, and with some of their publications. And when they commenced the publication of ,'The American Socialist'' I subscribed for it, and became a contributor to its columns. I combatted their claim that they had solved the labor problem. They said they were paying their employes about the same amount annually that they appropriated to their own use and thought that a fair division, the number of employes being nearly the same as the members of the community. I showed that the number of the former, only embraced the working force and that they had children and dependants which more than doubled the total. And that as far as the labor question was concerned the community was simply a corporation building up a large plant and pocketing profits from the joint production, in which the wage-workers had no share.

For a layman to attempt the discussion of a subject involving such intricate questions of Physiological Science and such complex problems of social ethics, may be deemed presumptious; but the observation and reflection of a long life, may enable me at least to attract the attention of those capable of doing it better justice. My apology is its great importance, and the importunate demand for light and wise counsel upon a matter, so closely related to the progress and happiness of the human race. With the theories of the Oneida Community or its practices in the relation of the sexes I can speak with little confidence. The field was new, the forces were subtle and under pressure of personal passions and public prejudices. That mistakes and disaster should attend it might have been foreseen. The facts of chemistry are sometimes discovered and often verified by serious and fatal explosions. Shall we therefore close the labratory and prohibit the use of the crucible? No principle involved in the improvement of human conditions but has its obverse side. Love, the prime factor in social life, is not an exception. It becomes in all of its forms either "a savor of life into life, or of death unto death," according as it is allowed its normal manifestation, and wisdom is exercised in apprehending and conforming to its complicated relations.

As stated by Shelley: "The whole of human science is comprised in one question: How can the advantages of intellect and civilization be reconciled with liberty and the pure pleasures of natural life?"

It is altogether impossible, it seems to me to formulate a system to be universally observed, even if such uniformity were desirable. The whole matter is subject to the great law of evolution and involves peoples and individuals in every stage of development. The eldest form of government known to history, is the Matriarchate, in which if monogamy or polygamy existed polyandry was the prevailing form. It exists in several countries to-day, and traces of it can now be found on every continent. and they are distictly intimated in the history of many races who claim monogamic marriage to be a divine institution, revealed especially to them. (see Gen. XXXVIII, Deut. XXV.) Monogamy instead of being of Jewish or of Christian derivation, as contended by the Church, was of pagan institution and to which the Jew and Christian were compelled to conform. Its purest form, embracing the home, and the developement of its nobler affections, was of German or Scandinavian origin.

The existence of sex and the mutual attraction observed in its manifestations constitute the paramount interest of human life. And it is for this reason that ecclesiastic and the civil ruler, have in attempting to guard it against the abuses and misdirections of ignorance, seized upon it as a sure means of perpetuating and extending their authority and power. They have invested marriage with forms of law and sacrament of religion, which so far from proving a guide and safe-guard to the weaker and unwary, has resulted through suppression of the natural impulses, which they have decreed to be vile and unclean, and the denial of opportunity for scientific investigation, in the vilest and most filthy abuses of the sex nature, and which the severest penal laws and sanctimonious denunciations, have not only failed utterly to remove, but have incalculably increased and perpetuated them far beyond what would have proved their normal limitation. Their pretentious legal sanctification of the passion, has not elevated but degraded it.

To remedy these results, mainly due as they exist to arbitrary repression and forceful invasion of personal rights and responsibility, more law of similar character is now demanded. Vice Societies are organized and incorporated to supercede the spy and detective work of the criminal law; heedless of the lessons of the past, and of the failure so patent, of its repressive force, even with its terrible death penalties for adultery and bastardy.

To the eradication of these evils, several movements have been inaugurated. The White Cross, the Social Purity advocates, seek to reform mankind with worthy aims, but with some loose philosophy and mistake of facts, which need revision. One mistake or oversight, into which nearly all writers on these questions have fallen, seem to have been made, by failing to distinguish between parental and conjugal love. Malthus treats overpopulation, as a product of the indulgence of the passions of mandkind, confounding sex attraction with desire for offspring, when in fact they have but remote relation to each other. It may be true, that in the primitive state with men, as still with animals, the sexual impulse serves merely "as a spur to propogation;" but as the race or individual advances, the connubial love developes a bond of mutual helpfulness and of enduring attachment, promotive of moral and spiritual growth. To ignore this fact leaves the human love on the same plane with the animal. Simple desire for offspring can have little to do with our present legal marriage. It does have a great influence over both men and women married or single, and affects their character to the extent it exists. But love of a fine establishment, of convenience and of social distinction, oftener than desire for children, or even the sexual impulse, is the ruling motive of the society woman, in the selection of a husband. Many couples could be found who have married with a mutual understanding that they were not to have children, at least for a number of years. Andrew Combe is said to have predetermined that matter, because, with all his great love for the woman he married, he was unwilling to transmit his defects of constitution to posterity. The purity advocates do not apply expressly the same rule to the legally married and to the legally unmarried. But purity is a principle not a creation of legislation. And yet even our medical writers speak of the same thing as pure or impure according to its place within or without the legal sanction, considering neither the health or cleanliness bodily or mentally of the parties. With this reckless disregard of the truth of things, the same act, which in the legally unmarried, is made debauchery, licentiousness and even rape, is pure and orderly, when according to the New Jersey Justice, no more force is used than is necessary to induce submission, on the part of the legal wife. The movement advocated by Alpha of which the late Dr. Caroline Winslow was a trusted leader, would exclude all intercourse except when children were mutually desired. This would of course prohibit all forced intercourse even to the legally married; but this to the average man and woman would not be regarded as marriage at all, since that is quite generally deemed to be a license to do what, without a license, is impurity, indecency and even crime. Diana, a pamphlet published by Mrs. Eliza Burns, undertakes to show that lovers may largely enjoy interchanges of affection, without proceeding to beget children, or to adopt the vulgar contracepts or any other of the devices to prevent conception, used largely now by married and unmarried people as well. Diana appears to complement Alpha.

"Karezza" by Miss Stockam, is still more explicit than Diana and shows, that very great intimacy may be enjoyed between the sexes, without the great exhaustion of nervous force, and waste of vitality, which attends reproduction, and that the intimacy so controlled, as to the married at least, becomes promotive of health and happiness and of exaltation of the moral nature. The point at which all these movements fail as efficient measures of reform, is that they only instruct the married as to how the sex nature may be orderly deleveoped, without the atrophy of disuse or dangers of abuse. The unmarried require knowledge as well. They may avail themselves of the knowledge conveyed to the married. But it will be only under the strain of a sense that such intimacy is wrong or thought to be wrong, and must be kept from the knowledge of all others. In time they may learn that the body is clean, when it is kept so as is the mind, when it is kept free from prurient imaginings and squeamish prudery. Mutual love alone sanctifies embraces and caresses. What that "has cleansed call not thou common or unclean!" Only Judas betrays with a kiss.

Proper knowledge and discipline would encourage earlier marriages for those who were unprepared to assume the responsibilities of rearing offspring, and so tide over the periods of greater impulse to yield to temptation and unchaste indulgence.

The existing feaful conditions, a conservatice Church and an invasive State have been increased and perpetuated in their efforts to correct the evils arising from the ignorance and superstition themselves have fostered. Any salutory reform must be gin with the enligtenment of the child, for long before either sex has reached adolescense certain habits may be formed and the mischief for life be done. The illregulated intercourse of the sexes, in or out of marriage, is but a small part of the unfortunate inheritance transmitted to us from past misdirection largely due to the separation of the sexes in early life; to monastic institutions; to a double and equivocal standard of morals; subjection of one sex to the other personally and economically, and to woman's social ostracism for an offense she had never been intelligently guarded against, and into which she may have been led by untimely yielding to natural impulse, or to hypnotic seduction. To these causes is due the desperate state in which many find themselves as to their sex life. Marriage has become, to them a failure, and life not worth living, to untold numbers married and single

Trials like those of Oscar Wilde and D. W. Corbett, give us occassional glimpses into the hidden vices which thrive under unnatural repression of sex attraction and the denial of scientific knowledge of life in its most intricate relations. Polygamy was responsible for this form. But can any one assure me that similar abuses of the sexual functions are not true as to the other sex?

The loathsome diseases which have proved so distructive to the life and health of soldiers and sailors, and been communicated to trusting wives and helpless children, has unquestionably resulted from the abnormal separation of the sexes, not from natural intimacy and intercourse. Sailors have been and still are separated for long intervals from any contact whatever with the opposite sex, and when in port only meet the lowest and most degraded. Only six out of a hundred of the British soldiers are allowed to marry. The rest must become ascetics, libertines, with almost a certainty of contracting disease, or abusers of themselves, which instead of incurring a specific disease destroys health of body and mind, begetting imbecility, idiocy and insanity. From these causes, our almshouses and asylums are largely peopled, not only with sailors and soldiers but with men and women who suffer in civil life.

I think few medical men will deny that they have patients of both sexes suffering from the consequences of the inversion of love and for the cure of which they prescribe marriage. Surely a disease which can be cured by the imparting of a little knowledge, would have been prevented by it.

In the existing condition of ignorance and prejudice it would not be practicable to withdraw the restraints now imposed by Church or State. "Martyrdom is the seed of the Church." It is of little value to science. Complete knowledge will lead to the choice of what is best, and those who will lead a true life will command respect and secure a following. To incite or encourage the ignorant and prejudiced, those who seek to own or destroy the one desired, to action upon matters or methods they cannot comprehend is to involve them in danger, do them a great wrong and at the same time to retard the triumph of the true principle of mutual and fraternal liberty. A strong sentiment is beginning to prevail among the equal rights women, and the advocates of chastity, that men and women should be mutually held to the same moral code. Many noble men favor the single standard. It does not appear what that may finally be. Whether that which male sentiment and male legislation has determined for woman, or that which it has indulgently allowed itself. Perhaps a compromise between the two. I think scarce a woman would be found to prescribe the narrow gauge for men, which they have allotted her, while herself claiming the broad license they have ever taken for themselves. Under the Hebrew law, the man could have wives, and concubines unlimited. But adultery was punished by death. Adultery for the man meant only an offence where the woman was another man's wife, his property. The woman could be divorced in a summary way, who did not "find favor in the eyes of her husband."

With the passing away of legal polygamy the treatment of woman became less oppressive; but virtual polygamy still exists among the most monogamic people. According to statements made by the purists, the houses of ill fame are patronized largely by married men in all countries prescribing monogamy. And of the married Christian statesmen who voted to kill Polygamy in Utah, many were known as patrons of the "pleasure houses" of Washington or keepers of mistresses. So far as the Alpha and Social Purity movements are concerned, not only must the man and the woman be held to the same standard, but also the married and the unmarried, in all matters of sex relation, unless exception be made in the rare instances where offspring are mutually desired. This may not be acknowledged by the parties, but is the stern logic of their position. The effect should these views prevail upon the legal marriage is not readily conjectured. But upon voluntary and mutual-love marriage its application is apparent. If mutual love is essential to marriage, when it ceases, marriage ceases.

That the monogamic marriage for life is the highest ideal of marriage is I think generally conceded, although, the need of a law to make it more so appears an admission to the contrary. We do not need a law to make water run down hill, or the sun to rise at a particular hour. And we do not make a punishable offense of attempts to ascertain the truth in these respects. But we can never know whether the monogamic life union is the highest and best form of marriage until the despotic hand of the state and the dogmatic dicta of the church shall be withdrawn from the trial balance, and the interested parties left free to determine it for themselves. The pure monogamic marriage has never been generally observed in any Christian country. The question then is not what form shall be arbitrarily established, but simply will freedom or despotism secure the greatest number of life long, happy monogamic unions? Through conventional legalities, the failure is all too patent. Freedom will succeed better. To doubt this is to abandon the pretension, and deny the monogamic claim altogether. All those who would separate but for the law, are already divorced as to any true marriage. •In reviewing the several forces which have already appeared in this controversy, I wish merely to forecaste the trend which the reform seems likely to take. Had my voice weight I would plead for freedom of investigation, and well ordered experimentation, under scientific conditions and tests, not only of this but of all subjects involving human well-being. As a matter of opinion I think that the lovemaking which becomes intelligent and in accord with the golden rule of "equal regard for others as for ourselves," marriage would not often prove the grave of love, but continue sweet, helpful and heathful to the end of life and the sex force cease to be either crucified or recklessly squandered in the early years, leaving life thereafter a blank and desolate barren to man and to woman, who desires the caresses of love long after the ability to bear children has lasped. It is the gentle bearing and fondling of the lover which wins and holds the affection of the true woman. It is only when the discovery is made that the husband cannot rise above what is low and animal in his love nature that there comes disappointment repulsion and disgust. When her love and intelligence is unable to lift and hold him to her level, submission becomes so humiliating and depressing that life is made a burden. But the tables are turned sometimes and the woman becomes the aggressive force. Unless the man can now lift her from the pool of sensuality this works a degeneracy as unfortunate as the other. She is not so constituted as to make physical force available, but by masterful will or hypnotic suggestion, she can work his ruin physically and mentally. There have been Antoninas in every age.

It is a hopeful circumstance that the movements to which I have referred are chiefly under the direction of women. In the differentiation of refined intercourse and mating for life from the mere animal function of reproduction, woman must necessarily take the lead and by her higher spirituality and truer social instinct save her brother and herself from the falses and misdirections, ignorance and long established habits have imposed upon their affection for each other.

The result of happily united lives in equal freedom, and equal regard for each other's well being cannot fail to reproduce offspring with healthful constitutions and noble natures. A marked advancement of the race may be anticipated from this source.

To show that woman has the higher appreciation of the principle of conjugal love, I will give an extract from an "Old Maid's" letter to a lady friend of mine, written nearly forty years ago.

"You want to know something of my heart life! As if old maids have any such or any hearts either! You believe it though! Well, if you had come to me in the Holidays you would have found me indulging in the painful luxury of reviewing the last ten years—of reading journals of that time—of persuing with tear-blinded eyes sweet letters dated long ago. Did I never relate to you the serious romance of my life? Never tell you that the gushing fountain of affection was first set flowing in 18— which keeps my heart warm yet, and beautifies every dry, dusty, withered thing I meet? But separation, followed by doubt and misgivings from opposition on the part of my friends, prevented our ever meeting again.

Necessity for actual exertion has sometimes dimmed my remembrances and blunted the keenness of my anguish—so saving me through these lonely years—for what purpose Supreme Wisdom only knows. I have loved if the special object has not been near. The "sweet waters of affectious spring" have been poured upon all about me, for I would not be selfish, and so lose the saving and sanctifying influence of love. Thank God! He has permittel me to taste it, though the sensuous draught is not for me. Yes! M! The living power of love has been mine. I see and feel how God can love his wayward, wandering children who have strayed. How love with self put aside, sanctifies, glorifies life, how even an old maid's inner life, aye! and outer too, can be made beautiful by love, how weak loving woman—strong in her weakness, learns, through her own passionate heart-beats, of the Infinite Law of Love upon which she leans, and of which through her own cravings she becomes conscious."

It may interest the reader to know that late in life when no probability of offspring remained, the writer of the above formed another, if less romantic attachment which proved happy and promotive of mutual and affectionate regard for more than thirty years.

Marriage may be distinguished as mutual, when of equals, or as possessory when of superior and inferior. The latter may be divided into such as predetermine the owner and the owned, and such as leave the determination of the question to the parties after marriage. It is conceivable that the mutual marriage may be orderly and helpful to both; that the possessory marriage, with the predetermined ownership may be orderly and helpful to the owner; but there seems little prospect of harmony while the struggle for mastery or ownership after marriage is going forward. When ultimately determined, however, the order of the militant type is realized, and ownership more or less complete becomes the status of the two in respect to each other. From this state arises, the jealous acrimonies, and antagonisms of married life, and the estrangements are unfaithfulness, so common in wedlock.

It is idle to think of rectifying these divergencies by restrictive laws and penal statutes. Larger liberty and the application of the Golden Rule only can bring those so circumstanced into apprecia- and antagonisms of married life, and the estrangements and unfaithful natures.

The tendency to co-education of the sexes from the kindergarten to the university, in schools of industry and manual training, and to co-work in most fields of activity, is truely hopeful, as is participation in healthful sports. Where division of labor is not clearly in-indicated by peculiar faculties or special adaptability the industrial co-operation of the sexes is promising. That woman is swinging back to equality with man in the external realm there can be no doubt. In proportion as equal freedom is attained, in opportunity and environment will mutuality become the rule of social life and the warfare of the races and of the sexes cease, in their insane attempts to capture and own or to destroy each other. Notwithstanding the intimate relation of this subject to all that concerns human happiness, I do not regard it as the fundamental social issue. The industrial and economic questions underlie it. Man and woman can only attain their highest development under equal freedom. In slavery, the purest love can only engender slaves. In an environment, from which they can be evicted and expatriated, or the products of their labors taken without return there can be no exalted social life for either. Given economic independence woman could

not be forced to assume or remain in relations distasteful to her or
suffer greatly from slighted affection, or unsuited companionship.
Instances are occurring even now where women with wealth in their
own name or with commanding talents in fields of literature, art
and industry, have taken independent ground and successfully defied the ostracisms of conventional society retaining the respect of
self and of friends. It is through her sense of financial dependence
and inability to support herself, that the mercenary or servile spirit
is developed in the frail woman and she sells herself for life for the
prospect of a home and of relief from the toil and care; or temporarily, for the means to satisfy her fancied needs or real hun-
ger. To make free the opportunities for renumerative employment,
should prove the surest course to redeem both Man and Woman
from the subjection and abuses they are mutually responsible for,
and which co-ercion of law or terrors of superstition have in all
the ages failed to remove.

CHAPTER XIX

In reviewing what has been written I find there are many tried
friends and some earnest opponents of the views emphasized in
these chapetrs, which have been omitted. In my denominational
relations, there was Zephemial Baker, Moses Ballon, Emmons Part-
ridge, E. E. Guild, W. M. Fernald and others. There were others
still, who were more particularly identified with the
spiritualistic departure. T. L. Harris, S. B. Brittain, Wm.
Fishbough, R. P. Ambler and many others to whom I
feel indebted for generous sympathy and wise suggestions. Dr. Brittain was a warm and dear friend of mine, when we were in the
Universalist fraternity, and our friendship remained through all
evolutions of progressive thought.

When that phenomenal book appeared, "Nature's Divine Revela-
tions," by Andrew J. Davis, I found myself in deep sympathy with
the persons who gathered around him. I had known Mr. Davis, when

a green youth, with neither culture not genius, aside from his clairvoyant powers. I had known Dr. Livingstone his first mesmeriser, and also Dr. Lyon, who mesmerised him while dictating the book. Mr. Fishbough the scribe, I had known for years. Neither of these were qualified to write a book like that. I was present during some of the sittings, and know that the things dictated were often a surprise to them all, and in conflict with their beliefs. This was particularly so with the scribe, who wrote as he was dictated to by the Seer.

As to the mystery of the book's production I am no better satisfied than at the time of its publication. Of the clairvount faculty of some minds I have no doubt, but of its extent and the reliance to be placed upon its communications, I have no decided notions. I feel certain that the book was produced as claimed. Once Metaphysical and speculative questions interested me, but on reading the book the "Voice to Mandkind" was the most attractive portion. It stated very clearly the social disorders of our industrial system and presented in very interesting form the system of Association of Charles Fourier. It prophesied that Peace, Plenty and human happiness should prevade the social world as soon as distributive justice should be established in the relations of human industry. After an address at Steinway Hall, by Wendell Philips, I heard Mr. Davis say to him: "The people who have declined for the last twenty years to listen to J. K. Ingalls, upon the land question, hear and think upon it now when you present the same subject and in the same way."

I may say here that in 1848 at an Abolition meeting in the Tabernacle, where Mr. George H. Evans had been given opportunity to speak on the land monopoly issue Mr. Philips had treated him in much the same way as Mr. Douglass did me, as stated in Chapter VII. Mr. Evans did not live to see Mr. Philips come to his position on the land question, as I lived to see Mr. Douglass come to mine; but he came to it quite as soon.

But with the limits permitted to this volume I am unable to notice many who have sympathized with me or who have opposed me in my advocacy of the "Use and Occupancy" title to land. The most direct way of attaining this desired condition has seemed to be the abrogation of all loans for the collection of rent. The same might be found necessary as to interest, or even profit, where the increase could not be shown to arise from some service rendered by the claimant.

I have had little to say about Trades Unions, not because I do not sympathize with the workingman; but because their organization is militant and only an antagonistic force.

Of course there can be no organization of industry, where the prime base is in the hands of private or corporate monopoly. To organize labor therefore is only intended to wage war on a field where all the material advantage is on the side of the monopolist. It can only be justified on the ground of absolute necessity.

I have many friends among the unionists. I will mention Victor Drury, C. Osborne Ward and Edward King; but I have always held that to attempt to prevent persons from working for any one on any terms which could be agreed upon, was one of the worst forms of tyranny that could be conceived. Were workingmen generally favorable to co-operation, and willing to accept the responsibilities of production and exchange, instead of the wage which transfers their shares in the joint increase, they could rightfully claim a share of the business from which they could not be discharged or evicted at the will of the employer, and have just and I think legal grounds for resisting any party who should attempt to take their job from them. A strike against wage work altogether would be intelligent and morally, justifiable. A strike for higher wages, or against a reduction of wages, is illogical while accepting the position of wage workers, and only justifiable as a war measure against positive or tacit combinations of employers. There seems to me little to hope from such measures. They can only in a very indirect way affect the land monopolist or the money manipulator who squeezes the employer and employe with equal zest and avidity.

That such organizations help on in a blind way the evolution of the industrial age is probable, if only through survival of the fittest by natural selection; but its advance through intelligent selection seems more desirable under the light which modern science social and economic throws upon the field of material prosperity and intellectual progress. Doubtless the tendency of workmen's com-

binations is towards the attainment of more exact knowledge. Their
disinclination to mass their forces in aid of partisan politics has
been favorable to deliberate thought and careful investigation of
principles, though their clannish tendencies have had an opposite
effect.

Within a few years past, I have become acquainted with the
literature of "The Labor Exchange," and have had slight correspondence with Carl Gleeser, F. W. Cotton, and others. Although
there is some discrepency between the regulars, who advocate a
general organisation, before attempting practical operations except
as experiments, and others who impatient of a deliberate and orderly advance, seek to rush into immediate demonstration, there is
little discrepancy, I think, in regard to the practicability of its
theory. So far as I am able to judge the theory is nearly faultless.
With its practical operation, or the wisdom being exercised in its
local management, I only am informed by reports, from time to
time published in the papers friendly to its purposes. Many mistakes and failures, will be met as a matter of course, but I see no
reason why with judicious direction it should not prove a means
of great good. It seems to embrace all the salient points of the
old Protective Unions, while avoiding their weak ones; giving to co-
operation its full scope in equitable exchange. As compared with
the other theoretical hobbies which distract the march of Reform,
or the remedies which enthusiasts seek to apply for the disease of
the social organism, it stands high above them all. Protective tariffs
quasi free trade, Land banks, Single Tax, Mutual Banking etc.,
have nothing in them of good which are not embraced in it, while
the fallacies of each are avoided.

Debt is eschewed. The labor check is redeemed by the thing for
which it was given or its approximate value in some other product
of labor. Thus the labor measure becomes the standard of value
in exchange, and a cornering of its money would mean nothing
but an unusual demand for labor; the only thing the laborer has to
sell. No serious defalcation or repudiation could take place without
involving a criminal act, and the temptation to such would be greatly reduced. This would be banking on a plenum not a vacuum.
But I by no means intend to say that as yet presented the Labor

Exchange is perfect. I have seen so many "schemes" in the last sixty years offered for the salvation of society, many of which worked directly to promote private advantage and the despoiling of honest industry, that I must ever accept with caution any plan which professes to work for the good of the toiling. Did the Exchange propose to bank on indebtedness as a means to benefit borrowers, I would shun it as I would the nightmare.

I will make but one criticism, not upon its potential capacity for good; but upon the advocacy of its principles, by those who antagonise the single tax, and the claims of the land reformers. It may be available to a plausible defense of the exchange to say it does not require political agitation or the making of laws to give it an impetus to success. I think also it might be advisable to confine its business at first to simple exchange and leave production to individual enterprise and initiative. But it will be found in the end or whenever the exchange enters the field of production in organised form, that the land question cannot be thus ignored.

Production is the first in order of the processes of increase. Division is second followed by exchange. Counters, money or checks are instruments in exchange. They are not essential to production or division. And can affect the equities of either in no conclusive way. To think of reforming either by manipulating the currency or exchange token is only the conception of a dreamer. He might as well think of cleansing the water of an impure spring by changing the bucket with which he goes for water.

Production of social wealth is through the associated labor upon the raw material, the land, either directly or through exchange. Now if the laborer or the land, are owned by a legal superior, the increase will be appropriated by the owner, and your division and exchange only concern him. What possibility is there then that the instrument by which exchanges are made, should secure justice to the worker in the matters determined befor the exchange takes place? But the value of the Labor Exchange principle can doubtless be demonstrated by experiments even under the operation of our pernicious land system. I prophecy that the Labor Exchange will be the first to acknowledge and adopt the labor hour as the true unit of commercial value, and its ultimate acceptance of occupancy and use as the only title to land ownership.

The issue between the organizers and those who favor immediate practical application of the principle and the individual iniative. I trust will not be serious or retard the progress of the work. A mutual and active co-operation of both sections is to be desired, which will not hamper the individual in the advocacy of private convictions, or the adoption of any principle of social science, discovered by any person interested in human progress.

With the state socialists, who promise to become a power in politics, a sort of forlorn hope to the populist advance, I have had little association. I believe most devoutly in co-operation, in Voluntary Socialism. But of co-operation under legal forms and compulsory processes we have altogether two much already. Our mammoth factories, our bonanza farms our department stores, furnish instances of most successful co-operation; but the principle of division being omitted or previously determined, exchange or its measures have no power to remedy the prior injustice. The experience of all time shows that collective rule develops all the evils which attends absolute personal government and that improvement has been gained mainly by relief of the individual from the spirit of invasion, whether from the monarch or majority. It was an ultra democratic jury which condemned Socrates to drink the hemlock. It was the voice of the majority that outweighed Pilate's impartial verdict when the Nazerene was sent to the Cross. It is the vote or the cowardly submission of the majority which establishes or allows to be established our syndicates and trusts and tolerates bribed legislators, corrupted officials and kept Judges. Not that these are worse than the average man or woman, but that the idea that one man or combination of men, may determine matters of interest to the life or possessions of the individual, destroys all sense of right and equity among men and makes the childish desire to dominate or rob others, a prime factor in all political and commercial affaris.

In the proper relation of the individual to the collectivity is to be found the solution of the industrial and every social question. To make the individual every thing and society nothing is absolutism and equal freedom becomes freedom for invasion. To make society everything and the individual nothing, ends in the same thing; completing the circle by reducing all individuality to subjection to the State, and then the State to the individual Paramount, who avers: "I am the State."

At present it appears that the fears of Herbert Spencer are well grounded, and that society has more to fear from centralization and authoriative socialism than from anarchist negation. To me it is evident that the motion of advancing civilization is vibratory between those two extremes, and that the mutual effort and not the extreme of either impulse should enlist our serious thought and action. Not liberty through order, or order through liberty: but liberty and order in Reciprocation of Service and Equity of Exchange.

APPENDIX.

The following Review appeared in Twentieth Century, 1890. It is in a line with my views of compulsory Socialism, and the primal relation of industry and economy. The two persons are representative men and are well known one as an admirer of Comte and the other of Rosini.

ETHICS AND ECONOMICS.

Prof. Thomas Davidson in the "Freethought Magazine" makes a metaphysical drive for "the source of economic law," and deems he has found it in the desire of the social aggregate, rather than in that of the individual man. He is indorsed in this by Mr. T. B. Wakeman in a late issue of Twentieth Century, who, never having seen one of the bovine species working singly, comes to the conclusion that "the teaminess of the ox" depends upon the yoke with which he is linked to others of his kind. To those who have enjoyed a wider observation, however, the "true inwardness" of the teaminess seems to depend on the individual ox, whether working with others or alone, or in whatever form of yoke. They think also that the horse, which works so efficiently in single harness, makes quite as good a representative of the toilsome burden-bearer as the ox. Although of somewhat different schools, this brace of philosophers appear to agree in imposing ethics arbitrarily upon economics, to correct and regulate it in those matters in which they deem it astray. Now, as little as I am disposed to defend "orthodox political economy," especially when it superciliously ignores and excludes its own fundamental principles, it seems certain that no generally recognized authority has ever justified Mr. Davidson's definition, that it "is the science of the gratification of unregulated desires for material things." For in this there are two unfair implications: first, that when economists pivot, as they now do, the whole science upon the question of value, and then define value as a thing depending on "a desire of the mind," they mean only a brutal and irrational desire. He is also mistaken in supposing that they recognize no desire but for material things.

I cannot call to mind an economist who has failed to point out that this estimate of value involves a rational appreciation of the uses of productive labor to promote the satisfaction of human love, especially the paternal, and of the social and nobler aims of life. Many values are determined, or greatly affected, even in present chaotic and barbaric trade by the degree in which they will minister to esthetic tastes, social intercourse and benevolent intent. Temperance increases the demand for bread and books as well as lessens that for whiskey. Should we define ethics, orthodox or otherwise, to be the science of the gratification of an unregulated desire for the coercion of human credence and for the arbitrary control of human conduct, M.r Davidson would doubtless think it unfair, while admitting that it but expresses the animus often actuating organizations for the promotion of morals and religion. He might insist that it was nevertheless in violation of the principles to which he proposes to subject economics. But the evils of our practical industrial and economic life, of which he justly complains, are mainly due, not to laissez faire, but to the disregard or evasion of it, through civil statutory legalities, interfering with freedom of opportunity, and enforcing idleness.

It is not to be denied that war, slavery and despotic governments have sometimes in a reactive way assisted progress, or that irrational liberty has sometimes degenerated into savageism; but the notable progress of mankind in all time has been linked to the broadest freedom, or to the struggles to attain it.

Now, morals and religion, let me suggest to these philosophers, are by no means the source of economic law, but are themselves the flower and fruitage of a tree from the root and branch of human industry and the reciprocal interchange of services and their equivalents. Social industry springs from the combined efforts of individuals to procure mutual satisfactions of human desires. The point at or upon which the physical and the psychical forces converge is "property." From this point we can proceed in our investigation into economic law without danger of plunging into physical abysses on the material side or of losing ourselves in the threadless labyrinths of metaphysical conjecture. We may thus escape the authoritative and approach an exact system of economy.

The great difficulty with our social studies is the equivocal nature of the terms we still so loosely employ. For instance, the term "competition "is used by the economists as the great regulator of human affairs, without which society could not get on at all. The same term is used by the Socialists as the very fittest to express all that is depraved and vicious in our industrial and business life. Yet if we search patiently the meaning each attaches to the word, we shall find they do not mean the same thing at all, but are pursuing divergent lines of thought, with no possibility of ever joining each other, or of even rationally attacking each other's positions. To economists the word means the pursuit by equals under freedom of opportunity. To Socialists it means the forced struggle of men barred from opportunity. To these it is not merely a striving for something for which others are also striving, but to which there is not freedom of access. To the others it is a seeking, though in rivalry, for something to which access is assumed to be free, and of which there is abundance for all. This is all wrong, says the Socialist; we must bring morals and religion and the law to regulate it. Keep out morals and religion, says the economist, and have law "let it alone;" the province of the law is to guard the "sacred rights of property," and to enforce contracts! Protect them, but let labor care for itself.

In truth the evils admitted more or less fully by both economist and Socialist are largely due to barbaric attempts of the past to impose morals, religion and law upon industry and trade. How much more of the same medicine will it take to cure the disease itself has caused? Does utter ignorance of a subject qualify one to dominate and rule it, and to direct "practical changes and legal measures," to thwart human desire and willing industry?

Whatever these philosophers may think I do not see it possible to study this planet from the center of the sideral system by looking in at the big end of the telescope. The earth has a measurable diameter and an orbit of its won. With these as units of measure we may proceed to survey the solar system with some prospect of accuracy, thence the sideral. "From the simple to the complex," is a maxim of positive philosophy. I think. We are in no position to synthetize until we have analyzed a subject. The principle ascertained in the minute primary leads on through every combination, however complex. The law which causes the falling apple to find its point of rest, seeking the straightest line and presenting the surface of least resistance to the obstructive medium: the plant to absorb the food within reach best calculated to promote its growth and prolong its life; the animal to obtain its forage with the least expenditure of force, is active in the man who seeks his individual good in wider fields and in the gratifications of more varied and refined desires.

If Mr. Davidson shall succeed in uprooting this selfishness from human nature he will at the same time uproot the source of ethical law as well, for utility is the primal law of ethics as well as of economics. For along this line flow all the refining and uplifting forces which work for good in every domain of human existence, partial or universal. The altruism of the positivist, as well as the reciprocity of the Golden Rule, measures duty to others by "love of self," for its personal satisfaction in its own fuller development and growth of nobler selfhood. And the still higher ethical motive, often acted on by the best and noblest of all time, yet never formulated in any organized ism, ethical or religious, the desire to make lighter and more fruitful the struggles of our continuous humanity in the time to come, is rich above all things in the gratification of truly human desire, though not unregulated, or particularly directed to material things. To the puerile comprehension which deems the germinating pulse perverse in thrusting itself above the ground instead of sending up the germ as other plants do, it will appear the proper thing to pull it up and compell it to grow after the orthodox mode. The success of the law-makers in rendering men religious by statute has not been marked. Nor has it been different in its attempts to make them more moral through compulsory processes. Notwithstanding all this it is thought that industry and commerce owe their very existence to statute law, or at least are mainly dependent on "legal measures." It may take some time yet to cure us of this stupendous stupidity, but until then sociology will be, practically, a figuring for the majority vote and the skillful running of the political machine.

It is far easier to speculate as to what "ought to be" than to carefully observe what is. Only on the latter basis can any exact science be founded. Perhaps the orbit of the earth ought to be a circle, and its plane coincide with the equator. But we have to deal with the facts as they are. Neither a plebiscite nor a "decree in council" will change them. It is in no sense different with the social movement or the evolution of economic law. Legislation to effect a change in that is but a "Pope's bull against the comet." Whatever it will bring to the Church or corporate exchequer will be missed from the wages of industry. This Mr. Davidson seems to apprehend when he asks: "Shall we legislate and combine in detail against the effects of the selfiesh principle?" and intimates that it might soonest correct the evil by leaving the "abomination unchecked," though he concludes on the whole that it is necessary to "go on applying legal plasters to the festering sores of society." But what if it be the legal plasters which produce the irritation and inflame the sores? Would it not be better to let Nature heal the sores?

We shall wait with patient curiosity while our philosophers "withdraw the whole of science from the domain of natural law and assign it to that of ethical law," that we may note the moral and sentimental tests and standards invented to replace the physical. As a measure of distance will the "golden rule" be applied, and the square and compass be superseded by "live of others." "Whoever would be greatest among you let him be your servant?" This last, by the way, we are told, "is the law of true, unselfish greatness." Is the desire then to be great, to attain a noble and well developed selfhood, unselfish? Though not to be classed with material things the satisfaction is personal. It does "not crush ambition," but changes its aim. We might conceive of the use of expletives and of sentimental phrases in place of thermometers, as it in any moment against his personal desire, selfish or unselfish. Is it that moral and sentimental education should be made, as he claims "the beginning, the middle and end of all education."

Were we to mention those who from the individualists' standpoint have promoted the intelligent appreciation of the good, in its ethical and universal sense, neither of the gentlemen I am criticising could be omitted. Not only do they belong to recent schools of thought, but each is an independent thinker in his particular school. Neither Comte nor Rosini are accepted by either as the "end of the law." Systems are modified by the individual thinker. It would be a brave organizer who would attempt to yoke either of these men in any movement against his personal desire, selfish or unselfish. Is it certain, then, that when individual effort in the higher sphere of labor has had salutary results freedom of effort in the humbler sphere should work only dire calamity? It is certain that the few whose organized rapacity seeks to rule by "legal measures" and by false education, through control of State and Church, studiously deceive and mislead the unorganized layman in respect to the tendencies of economic law, and that to this cause the great evils of our social and industrial life is due, and not to any rational application of that law or of personal liberty. Men seek by preference what is good, and would do right under the ethical law, but for their failure to grasp intellectually the economic sequence of their actions, and which moralists seem less able to understand than the unscrupulous. It is not, therefore, so much a lack of moral education and of a disposition to co-operate, which all human experience tends to promote, as of a knowledge as to what is conducive to personal or public good. Ignorance of economic law is the prime source of evil in every phase of the social life. It leaves ethics without motive.

THE LABOR HOUR—ITS PLACE IN ECOMICS.

The Force which moves all useful things from a state of rest or equilibrium into that of active circulation to serve the needs of human society has for its unit the Labor Hour. By the discovery, capture, transportation and preperation for consumption of all desired things, it procures every form of social wealth. With its passive complement the land and the natural forces and growths it is the source from which all increase arises and by it the normal price of serviceable things is determined. The co-operative labor hour, with wise specialization of its work, and equitable division of its products measures the value of all desirable productions.

After wealth has been produced and justly or unjustly shared among the co-operators, there arises a necessity of exchange. In fact an equitable exchange is the highest form of co-operation, since persons then are co-operating, though at the most diverse employments, and at the utmost distances from each other.

The earliest form of co-operation, and indeed of exchange, is where the service of one is balanced by the service of the other; as where pioneers assist each other in rearing cabins, clearing forests, breaking refractory sods, etc., and where return of service is made in kind. In all these transactions, the hours and minutes wrought determine the measure of reciprocal service; nothing else can. When the services are of marked inequality as to strength or efficiency of the labor, they are usually modified by a ratio of efficiency, respectively to the parties.

The earliest exchange of labor products is Barter, where the things desired are directly exchanged; and which though most convenient, where two meet who have the exact things needed by each the equity of the transaction may be quite difficult of determination. To facilitate and make more equitable exchanges in a wider circulation, intermediary measures have been sought. When labor was thoroughly enslaved, of course little attention was paid to the element of time or intensity of labor in the products exchanged; but when various industries came to be followed by freemen, a day's or hour's labor was more readily appreciated. Indeed an argument in favor of gold as a basis of currency has been made that its coins merely expressed in a general way the day's or hour's labor spent in its production. Upon the truth of this loose assertion depends all the claim the ounce of gold or silver has to be regarded an honest medium of exchange, a just basis for all kinds of currency, and of all promises to pay, used as currency. A century and a quarter ago, even when slavery was common in most Christian countries, Adam Smith gave to the world his apothegms: "Labor was the original price paid for all things, and labor is the ultimate thing satisfying all demands;" no more or less true because he said it, nor because Macleod has attempted to belittle it by showing that many other sources besides labor are the cause of the value of things: instancing, copyrights, Patents, funded debts, advowson, etc., and he could have added with equal truth, a letter of Marque, a license to keep a brothel, a gambling hell, or "fence" for stolen goods, or any exclusive franchise of arbitrary law, devised to take money from one man's pocket and put it into another's. But such things have no place in positive economics. Legal money and legal enforcements of contracts of indebtedness, can subvert all values and all units. They make the laborer, or the product of his labor, the property of a superior, whose will, fiat or "command to an inferior" determines both division and valuation.

In several essays in Twentieth Century and other journals I have demonstrated in the face of caustic critisism that there are two distinct rents, profits or interest, i. e. increments of wealth. The one, the normal increase of the season's industry, under free economic conditions; the other, the invasive force of the superior over the laborer or over the product of his labor. I now propose to show that there are two kinds of money. The one discovered and applied under freedom in exchange, the other the creature of law. The former facilitates the completion of exchanges. The latter obstructs exchange and defers its completion, putting off satisfaction, indefinitely and inviting invasion on the one side and repudiation on the other. By treating these monies as identical, we confound the mutual money of equals having honest intent, with the money of superior and inferior, contrived for spoliation and to justify subjection, and to capture the increase labor has earned. Reform under such relations is impossible. This is seen in the contentions between the several camps of the currency reformers. Mono or bimetalism, legal tender paper, fiat, warehouse certificates, labor checks, etc., all are advocated zealously as panaceas. This diverts our minds from the tyrannous laws which confound authoritative money with the free money of commerce which seeks to distribute equitably the increment of wealth; but which the legal accumulators of wealth seek to prevent by every legal dodge and by laws enacted in their behalf; so that it becomes difficult to draw the line between the money which aids and the money which hampers production: between that which effects prompt completion of exchanges, and that which defers their completion forever. And this is because money is regarded as a concrete thing, as a certain weight of gold or silver, and not as an abstract unit of force, or of purchasing power.

Legal money, coined by government, with power to "fix the value thereof"; to create bonds and debts; to bind creditors under forfeitures and penalties, to return it plus the use or increase which labor may be able to realize from its employment, benefits labor in no way, facilitates satisfaction in exchange in no respect and only benefits the increment capturer, who by aid of law simply exacts by its agency the same proportion of the social increase as the landholder, or the man who lets plant and machinery to the user.

The labor hour produces increase by arithmetical ratio of one. Legal money by a geometrical ratio of two. This distinction between the honest money of equitable commerce and the brigand device for the capture of labor's increased earnings, no student of social science should allow to escape him. But in the discussion of kaleidoscopic values, measures and standards, ideal and concrete, the wide chasm opening before us of poverty and want is unnoticed, or only regarded as the work of a mysterious providence. It is the mystery of the financial juggler, and for him truly a bountiful providence.

It is a feature of the gold basis and legal tender scheme, that while debts can be contracted and charged up for any and every commodity whatever, and indeed for their "creation out of nothing," only one commodity can serve as money of redemption from debt. Debt is thus a vast pen, with doors opening inward for such as will offer to become hostage for the redemption of the accumulating "evidences." There is however only one door opening outward, by which exodus is possible, the gold door. There are inner doors, of silver and of paper apparently opening outward to those who seek exit, but which only lead to the golden gate the only door of deliverance. Is it any wonder so many panics occur, and so many fail to get out and are crushed and die in debt! Surely there should be no commodities with ability to create debt, which are not competent to discharge it. If free Banking will not release the debtor from debt, how can it release him from paying interest? If it will release him from debt, will my friends tell me what need we have for a mutual bank more than for a mutual admiration society.

To overcome the difficulties of barter is the sole function of the commercial counter or token. It is simply a labor saving device to reduce the labor of bringing a large number of persons and commodities together as in a fair. Its costs and its benefits can all be measured by the labor hour with approximate exactness, beyond which the exchange of commodities makes no pretension of going. Parties may exchange commodities of like nature and quality by exact ratios, as of one ounce of silver or of gold, for another ounce of same. But there being no advantage personal or reciprocal in such transaction, it is not likely to occur, and has no scientific importance. There could be no call to exchange with an invariable standard.

To remonetize silver and give it free and unlimited coinage will only broaden the base of the legal tender inversion, and may enable the debtor to pay his interest and perhaps a little principal in cheaper money. But it will also enable the creditor to correspondingly broaden the base of his tribute bearing credits. The demand for mortgage secured loans will increase and which will be pressed for settlement when currency again becomes scarce and dear.

With paper money on a metallic basis the expansive and contractile force of the currency is greatly increased and which as Mr. Kitson in his book clearly shows is the feature most injurious to the debtor, the spreading and closing of the net which captures the increase and destroys the debtor. This force, the ability to expand and contract the currency, is wholly in the hands of the creditor class, who control the action of all governments on all financial questions. Only in exceptional cases can it favor the debtor. The legal tender paper or fiat money, only increases that force, and intensifies the panic when it is precipitated by intention or circumstance, or when the utmost limit of the expansion has been reached. Yet

blatant pretenders to a knowledge of monetary science sagely talk
of the functions of money and of the standards and measures of
value, without giving us the least clue as to whether they mean
the money of the government licensed brigand, or the money of re-
-iprocal commerce.

Not until this distinction is apprehended can it make any radical
difference whether transactions are carried on with a pound of tobac-
co, and ounce of silver or penny weight of gold, a check for a labor
hour, or for an ideal unit of purchasing power, as a standard. The
man who pays Nature's price labor for the increase he has procur-
ed will be in no wise benefitted, if he belongs to the inferior, the
debtor class. The superior, the creditor, captures it as soon as obtained, with all the avidity the eagle displays in pursuing and captur-
ing the booty the osprey has just lifted from the waves.

Our present dollar is sufficiently ideal and more elastic than
caoutchouc. Within the generation scarce passed, it has consisted
of 25.8 grains of gold, 10 grains of gold; 420 grains of silver, 412 1-2
grains Silver 375, 180 and 150 grains of silver at one and the same
time. It would buy 1 bushel of wheat, 12 quarts of wheat. It would
in 1895 buy nearly two bushels of wheat, either the "full legal
tender," or the 50c. half legal tender dollar or the circulating promise to pay either. Either now will buy ten labor hours of the ditcher
or scavenger or of other sellers of useful service. It will buy an
hour's service of a favorite clerk or salesman, twenty minutes of a
bank or rail road president, a few seconds of a multi-millionaire at
the questionable service of coupon clipping.

Mr. Tucker, prominent as a leader of Philosophic anarchism, in
the face of these disparities, asked me some years ago, if I "would
abolish money." And when I answered: "Yes! legal money," he
did not deem it worthy of notice yet reprinted the question and
omission in "Instead of a Book." And yet he with Mr. Bilgram, Mr.
Westrup and even Mr. Kitson regards the money question the all
engrossing economic issue, and the increase of debt as the only
means of escaping its penalty; reminding one of India. *

Mr. Westrup suggests that if I have a plan to restore equity and
mutualism to commerce I should make it known. Well! I have none.
If however, we will remove the cause, the invasive laws and control

of the government, its enforced collection of interest and rent indebtedness, commerce will take care of the facilities and equities of exchange, and find a good enough unit of value or purchasing intermediary.

Abolishing forcible collections of rent, leaving economic and voluntary rent to take care of itself, and doing the same with enforced and voluntary or economic interest, money will become as harmless and unimportant an instrument of exchange, as yard sticks and quart pots now are in retail trade. Were the keys of our houses and treasury chests, put under government regulation, and a franchise given to a syndicate to manufacture and sell or loan them; we might be imprisoned in our homes or locked out of them, and from our valuables, without the least redress and they would become the most valuable thing in use. Make such manufacture and sale free from forceful control, and the key becomes an insignificant though immensely useful affair. It would be the same with money. Was the forcible collection of rent of land abolished, it would greatly but not wholly reduce the rent of capital. To abolish rent of capital, would not in the least affect the rent of land. Were the laws enforcing interest abrogated, all involuntary payment of interest would cease. Would equal freedom then require that voluntary payment of it should be prohibited when the borrower imagined that the lender had done him a service, or added to his acquirement?

Our finance reformers generally admit that our monetary laws are at fault, yet appear to agree with the "pure economists," of the Macleod school who make exchangeability the sole feature of economics, ignoring production and division; and treat money as the first and greatest of the economic forces, and not as it normally is, when not regulated by government, the last and least. The treasure chest and home have becoms second in importance to the key, when the key commands access to them and is in the keeping of the superior.

The discussion between these gentlemen interests me only as matters of metephysical speculation. It is vain to seek an invariable unit of value, ideal or concrete. (It would exchange nothing if found. One or both parties profit by a trade.) Only a rational approximation to equity can be obtained. That a single commodity cannot be an exact or even tolerable standard, Mr. Kitson has demonstrated beyond all doubt. Only a commodity which would satisfy all human desires, rational and irrational, could be an exact measure, and gold or silver satisfies only a few trivial wants and they not among the most rational. As money they are desired in trade because they can command the product of the labor hour, or rather its increase over expense. This then is the ideal commodity which serves to satisfy all material human desires; and becomes a near approximation to an exact medium or measure of exchange in the order of reciprocal transfers, and the last thing paid in satisfaction. The Pioneer exchanges hour's and day's work with his neighbor in rolling and burning logs in the clearing; in joining teams at heavy breaking,etc. These exchanges of service are necessarily made in terms of the labor hour; and which so far as the utilities and measurement of time are concerned, are ascertainable with mathematical exactness. The energy and intensity or effectiveness of the labor only will vary; but this variation can be calculated with tolerable correctness except as to the respective necessities of each person at the time. In this illustration is embraced the whole matter of exchange and its varying values, prices, and the purchasing power of things. Bastiat's statement, that we only exchange services is true, notwithstanding the absurd purpose to which he put it; viz.: That the accrued increments of wealth are due to service rendered by the legal owner, or by his ancestors or donors. Had he added, or by their inferior tenants, or slaves it would be true. It more truly demonstrates that they are due to the robbery of the holder or of his ancestors or donors!

But whether the commodity standard, or the unit of invariable purchasing power is the better term for the intermediary of exchange, is unimportant, so long as forceful laws compel payments of rent of land, rent of capital or rent of ·money, or fulfilment of contracts of any kind to defer completion of exchanges, or which are tainted with inequity. Submission to these laws means perpetuation of "interest for the use of capital," which these friends are so anxious to kill, and which they are confident a mutual bank, or an ingenious device of some kind with or without a standard will unavoidably effect. Yet they retain the bonds of contract, the death pledges of deferred payments, and the essential spirit of the old barbarism of superior and inferior, with unilateral rights on one side and unilateral duties on the other; the right to command and the duty to obey, the right to take and the duty to yield. Should not a man be required to pay his debts? But agreement to defer a settlement is not payment of a debt and cannot be had without paying usury, its natural and legal penalty. To recognize contracts defering payments is not only recognizing usury but establishing it. It certainly is a strange way to kill it.

Now each of the reformers to whom I have referred except Mr. Bilgram, is silent about calling in the power of the government to enforce usury bearing contracts. He assumes that contracts made where one man's hour is valued equal to 2,000 of other men's hours or ten years of arduous service and where idleness of a part is involuntarily compelled by class domination of the complementary factor of production, are made under "equal freedom" and that the man who fails in fulfilling its conditions is an invader and to be treated as a criminal. And with the others there is an unsatisfactory non-commitalism. If they do not endorse the "sacred contract" superstition, they to a certain extent ignore the subject.

Of course if age could make the contract sacred, it is eminently so. It has constituted the legal prop of slavery in every age. Through the centuries it has stood unquestioned in jurispendence, except in sporadic cases, where a Solon, a Mansfield or a Haliburton, has interposed a word of equity, collapsing the "fiction of law," which held the slaves or "mortgaged lands and citizens" in bondage.

Within the last half of this century, it held four millions of people as bondmen to superiors, slave holders, in this republic. It still holds ten times that number of dependent people, tenants and hirelings, under tribute to land holders, bond and mortgage holders less regardful of the humanities or of the sense of justice, than ever characterized other than the lowest and most brutal type of slave holders.

One may get goods of another without anything to pay for them. This is no invasion, unless he uses force or fraud in obtaining them. If otherwise lending and borrowing becomes a venture in an untried experiment, of pure hazard. Only as a venture has it any place in economy. Then it becomes a partnership or matter of co-operation, where risks are mutual, the capital of the lender, against the unearned increment of the operator. There is no cause of action here, except some violation of equity be found. Comrades will hardly interfere to prevent or to enforce contracts of pure hazard. To do so would benefit no one but Shylock or frauds or blackmailers. Was the labor hour recognized as the money of redemption in law as it is in fact, the enforcement of contracts would give the laborer employment instead of depriving him of it, as now. Under Chattelism, their were no tramps in search of work; but sometimes "fugatives from labor."

Under legal enforcement of usurious contracts it is quite true that "money has a tendency to concentrate in few hands." Without such laws it is equally clear to me that the economic tendency would be to disperse, as well as concentrate, the money of commerce, whether contracted or expanded in volume. It should be equally clear that the only rational method of counteracting the tendency to concentrate wealth- prejudicially is to abolish such laws.

Facility for exchanging commodities does not largely depend on plenty or scarcity of money. It is certain that in the absence of legal money exchanges would be more readily effected than now. There is no legal money in international trade. Gold is estimated as bullion, not by the stamp at all; and yet it is deemed necessary to make tariff and excise laws to prevent exchanges being too easily made.

It is the incurring and discharging of debts alone which makes contraction and expansion of the currency disastrous. Loans of money or of goods are not completed exchanges. Credit is often a mere charity and as often promotes idleness or reckless speculation as industry. It is a law sanctioned vice. Usury is its inevitable sequence, is the penalty for deferred payment, compounded in advance by the creditor at a stipulated rate to the detriment of the public weal and public morals. Why should the creditor be protected in this business, and the debtor be treated as a felon?

To enforce contracts of this nature promotes the concentration of wealth in a few hands and the exploitation of the industries. Without this law created power the usurer could not collect his "tribute from the producer," the landlord involuntary rent from the tenant, nor the speculator profit from his burden bearer.

Usurious contracts are usually (not occasionally) made under duress. Threats of eviction, loss of home, business, and opportunity to work are quite effective to compel consent, and safer for the robber than revolvers. Usury and bankruptcy are the inseperable sequences of credit under laws for the enforcement of contracts, because such laws encourage idle and vicious and gambling bargains, but have little effect in preventing purposed defalcations.

It might be interesting to inquire what would occur should interest on money, by any device be reduced to zero, under existing laws. Such money could buy no land or productive property of any kind. Nothing yielding increase would be exchanged for money yielding no increase. This subject is greatly misconceived by both the usury and the anti-usury advocate. The source of usury is not long or short money. It is the ability of labor to procure more things, which are objects of human desire, than it consumes; and it exists, whether there are landlords, usurers and profit mongers to capture it from the worker or not. Laws for the forcible collection of rent, interest and speculative profits simply confer a privilege to a class to take the increase of labor's production, which would otherwise remain in the possession of the purchaser. To repeal these laws should seem to be a sensible method of correcting this universally acknowledged evil. Our great monopolies of land, money and trade are powerful for evil, only because they have a government of force behind them to compel payment. To abolish the law for the collection of rent would set free the use of land and render the landlord useful; of interest would set free the use of money and make the banker helpful; of speculative profit would set trade free and add the speculator to the producing class.

Thus the sharing of the economic increase would become a matter of equity instead of spoliation. Now it is more subject to the law of force, than to the economic law. The collection of strictly business debts would be a matter of secondary importance, treated as a civil or as a criminal issue. Few debts are now incurred except under duress, from conditions created by the enforcement of the legal fictions which give sanction to the claim of landlord, usurer and profit hunter. The making and renewing of contracts are thus compelled, and extra usurious rates or bonuses are accepted to escape the consequences of previously existing vicious bargainings.

Strictly business debts are in comparatively small amounts, and are of temporary and fluctuating operation, as often on one side of the business ledger as the other, the debt falling normally where the increased wealth is held, so equalizing its distribution. The distribution by force tends ever one way, to gather as tribute, the productive increase from those who produce, to those who capture it. Our debts for which we have received nothing absorb more annual interest than our imports on foreign productions yield, and probably more than our entire exports.

Would it not be more wise to abolish these force laws then to invent or multiply tools which can be made more effective still for accumulation?

* General Booth found that India is a great pawnshop. The people put in pledge their lands, oxen, jewelry, themselves, their children and their grandchildren. Their ideas of finance are crude, and they seem to think that he is the cleverest man who finds the largest number of ways by which to borrow money.—New York World.

DOMINION OF THE LAND.

Next to the man, the active factor in the social industry of the world, and complemental in every phase of productivity, is the Land. In this term is included all material, and every force and opportunity available for satisfying human needs and gratifying human desires. From this great storehouse of Nature are drawn all forms of wealth. From it man supplies himself through the exercise of his activities with food, shelter and raiment, and so makes human existence and social growth possible. Dominion of the land is then a fundamental element in social industry and forms the material basis of all civil rule and of all economic relations. In primitive states this truth was only partially apprehended, but even the mere hunter soon found it necessary to assume boundaries to his hunting grounds, which strangers might not invade to lessen his scant and precarious means of supply. Then tribes combined to guard their hunting grounds, though as yet their wandering life was confined to no located homes or exact limits. And when territory of a particular tribe became determined, there would still remain large ranges of "debatable land" between the different tribes. With advancing cultivation of the soil, habitation became fixed. Within the tribe or primitive village, each family had equal opportunity and use of land. Traces of this form of holding still survive among all historic peoples. The separate nation still claims exclusive dominion over its own territory and the control of fisheries adjoining its coasts. The people generally enjoy a common right to fish and to gather other products yielded by the sea. Bivalves, sea-weed, wild fowl, etc., are common property, or more exactly common opportunity. Even the right to hunt inland game on a neighbor's domain is acknowledged in the absence of statute law. The cultivation of the land begat a more stable means of support, and wrought a great if gradual change in industrial life, and made necessary settled abodes and the reduction of the area allotted to the support of the family or tribe. Separateness as to the home, became at once more marked although the common fields would be still worked in common, the produce of which would be common property. From this followed allotments of land for private cultivation. These were made changeable, and were required to be cultivated in rotation as with the general domain. This, in the absence of exact science, was the wisest method of tillage, and according to M. Laveleye is still followed in so densely a populated country as Belgium. To this writer, to Henry Summer Maine, Von Maurer etc., the reader is referred for a clear statement of the origin of land tenure. That an orderly development of natural ownership did not continue, is due to the supremacy of the despotic and militant spirit which intervened to break up and reduce to subjection, the primitive tribal commune. The simple common right had become detached to a separate holding or occupancy. It is evident little social progress could have been made without detaching the individual ownership from the common dominion. As population increased and industries became specialized, individual control of the land could not have been avoided, outside of a despotism as complete and as beneficient as that of the Peruvian Incas. The "shifting severalties" would become fixed. Some members would migrate and others obtain subsistence by resorting to handicrafts, and others offer service to more thrifty and enterprising neighbors. It was thus that the private appropriation of the land grew. The principal features of that early tenure still exists. Aside from statute law and those shallow fictions which our courts still hold to be above constitutions, they must prevail. Repeal the laws evicting the cultivator from his home, and enforcing collection of rent tribute, occupation would be left the only title in the separate control, while opportunity for common access to land would still be enjoyed.

The people to whom we are indebted for the civil law, the Romans have left us the elements of a system of property, which has stood the test of centuries of revolution and of the changing forms of government and of society. Let us see to what extent this law can be disentangled from the fictions which fendalism and authoritative systems have thrown around it. In Ancient Rome, the family was ruled by an absolute despotism. The father had full power of property over his household; of life and death over his wife, children and slaves; but at the same time was on a strict equality with all other householders, united under a common ancestor; the state consisting of a number of tribes or gentes, families of ten. To each householder there was assigned the dominion of a small allotment of land, which at first scarcely exceeded one acre. As with the "Mark" of the Tentonic villages, the common lands were pastured and to some extent cultivated in common, and the state held control of all outlying lands. These were partitioned off as required for use, or rented to meet state exigencies. Here appeared first the encroachment which ultimately proved so pernicious to the people, and finally destroyed the nation itself, that insidious power of wealth, which in defiance of both the letter and spirit of the primitive law, made laws of its own to disinherit and evict the Roman citizen. And similar processes seem to have obtained among all socities passing from a common to a separate ownership.

Now the absolute dominion of the primitive Roman law embraced only the domicil, the domain of the parent, on the principle that "the house is one's castle." The dominion of the village over its domain, was in its collective householders. The domain of the state was, theoretically at least, in its people, however delegated. How the dominion of one person first became extended over the homes of many, history gives but vague intimation. The differing systems of ownership evince little rational sequence, and are wholly without ethical or economic justification. Extended private dominion rests wholly on "right of conquest," the "law of the stronger." This is good against the weakest until he becomes the stronger, or a stronger than either comes. To guard the citizen against such encroachments, Rome instituted her

AGRARIAN LAW.

It was to enforce this organic law, and not as Neibhur claimed, merely to correct abuses in the administration of the public lands, and to enforce the payment of rents from wealthy tenants, that repeated attempts were made to effect salutary reforms in the national land policy. In these efforts, Servis Tullis sacrificed himself. Already a broad enlargemet of private dominion had taken place, the dominion of the home had grown from one to a round dozen acres, and for the equestrian order, a much larger acereage. Registration became established as soon as dominion exceeded possession or occupation; and the usurpation became protected by the state. In the time of the Gracchi, dominion of land in excess of occupation had become absolutely unlimited as with us. This had been done by the intrigue of the wealthy appropriators of the Ager Publicus, to enable them to employ ever increasing numbers of slaves; but in defiance of public law as it was of the public welfare. Each large proprietor came to have his retainers and tenants, as well as slaves. His original family domicil became a lordship's domain. The slaves tilled the ground and did most of the mechanical labor, while Roman citizens could occupy their national domain only at his will, and by paying tribute to him.

The only other resource was to take service in the army. All ordinary opportunities were closed to them. Thus the army ultimately became filled with mercenaries, who retained no stake in the national prosperity. Both the free population, despoiled of land, and the slaves, despoiled of personal liberty, increased greatly in each generation, until the barbarians appeared befor the gates of Rome, when there was found neither strength nor courage to defend her. It was not, as Macleod asserts, because "Her yeomanry of the bright days of the republic had perished in her foreign wars." Her population had not decreased. The Roman matrons were ever fruitful. It was because her people had been displaced, disinherited, evicted from their lands and homes, through maladministration of the land, which at the same time exhausted the fertility of her soil and the manhood of her sons.

It was an Italy thus given up to the despotism of greed, that Spartacus found so favorable for the most brilliant servile insurrection of all time. Of this era it has been said: "A great portion of Southern and Central Italy, especially, had been turned into pasture land, and instead of villages of sturdy and independent farmers, who owned the land they tilled (as in former times) gangs of discontented slaves, watched the flocks and herds of great nobles, demoralized by the plethora of illgotten riches."

The manner in which the citizen became reduced to the condition of a serf, is clearly yet briefly stated by Professor Ramsey in "Roman Antiquities."

"The Ager Publicus having been acquired numerous abuses arose in process of time, especially among tenants of the second class, these being, in the earlier ages, exclusively patricians, who at the same time monopolized the administration of public afffairs, were in the habit of defrauding the state, either by neglect altogether to pay the stipulated proportion of the produce, or by paying less than was due, or, finally by claiming what was Ager Publicus as their own private property. * * * Meanwhile deficencies in the public treasury were made up by heavier taxes, and the plebians complained that they were impoverished by new imposts, while the lands belonging to the community, which they had acquired by their blood, if fairly managed would yield a sufficient return to meet all demands upon the exchequer; or if apportioned out in allotments among themselves would afford the means of supporting the increased burden. * * * It is true the wealthier plebians soon also became tenants of the ager publicus, but though this circumstance materially strengthened the hands of the occupiers, it did not improve the condition of the poor or make them feel less keenly alive to the injustice of the system against which they protested." Niebhur and Dr. Arnold have mistaken the tendency of estates to increase under limitless extension of property beyond possession or occupation as a veritable "law of property." But those great estates, which ruined Italy, were not acquired under any law of property, ever recognized as rational or equitable by Roman or barbarian. The only legal justification they ever received, was through the most flagrant disregard of the principles of law by organized or tacit conspiracies to defraud the people, at the same time out of their inheritance and of their citizenship. Dominion of the land is the basis of all political power, of all sovereignty, whether of the monarch or of the individual. Without equitable dominion of the land, equality of citizenship is impossible. The large proprietors fully understood that their landed possessions were fictitious, fraudulent and indefensible; that they were the fruit of bribery, betrayal of trusts and as destructive of exact laws of property as of the public weal. It is humiliating to note the subordination of such intellects as Arnold's and Niebhur's to a shallow fiction, whose prenicious power no historian has failed to characterize and no sophist dared to defend. The noble Romans, noblest in all history, who gave their labor and lives to stay the tide of this devastating flood, need not appologies from schooled ignorance. They held themselves loyal to the public weal, the "higher law" of public life. They were mainly of patrician blood, and their manly conduct stands in vivid contrast to that of those wealthy plebians, who took advantage of the clamors of the populace only to improve the opportunity to make better terms with the oligarchy and to buy into the privilege and place, where they might share the plunder of a ruined people.

It is true these estates, under a class regime had obtained all the potencies of a principle of property as these more modern apologists suggest. Quite as truly, under the same rule and by the same logic, men and women were at the same time held as property, and continued to be for twenty centuries in all civilized states. The law for chattel slavery is more ancient than that for vacant land ownership, and quite as logically or economically justifiable; but no moralist of note and no economist of distinction, has attempted to justify or seriously attempt an apology for it, since the days of John C. Calhoun.

Land, other than what is occupied and used by one, is, in no scientific sense, property. Ownership of it is dominion, and no other right is exercised over it. Buying and selling of it is simply dealing in a royal prerogative, the right to exclude or to collect tribute, "royalty" (rent). One person having dominion over the home of another is empowered to collect tribute, as one nation extending its domonion over another nation does. There is nothing in it which answers the conditions of property. There is no "sacred" principle of private property," or of human right or of equity, which it does not violate: no true property which it does not imperil confiscate or exploit.

Really the plan in operation in Rome, through nearly its whole history, and which culminated in the Latifunda that ultimately strangled the national life, was in the main the same as that recommended by Henry George. From "nationalization of the land" and renting by the state arose the fearful abuses and large estates which ruined Rome.

It is evident, I think, from what here appears that private ownership of land beyond what is occupied and used, can in no true sense be termed "property." It is when so created by statute dominion and has more of a political than an economic or civil significance. One nation having dominion over the land of a sister nation, has the power to exact tribute. So one man having dominion over the home of another does the same—exacts rent. It is simply impossible to form an equation out of such transactions by any normal economic or equity rule. And there is nothing in such dominion which relates to any principle of property.

Property is defined to be "the right to be protected in the product of one's labor"; or to the "ownership of that to which one's labor is joined." Neither of these principles apply to a non-occupying dominion of the land.

For such land is not "the product of one's labor.

It is not a thing "to which one's labor is joined."

It is the natural inheritance of the first occupier.

It is not subject to be moved and carried away by one.

It is naturally inexhangeable with human labor.

Where existing by statute or custom, it is upon the false assumption that the landlord is in possession, when not he but the occupier is in possession.

Our own country is traveling rapidly the way of ancient Rome. Its public domain, though acknowledged by politicians to be "a trust to be strictly administered for the use of the people in coming generations," has been corruptly given over to large corporations and to the spirit of conscienceless speculation. There is only one course to save it, the recognition of occupancy as the sufficient and only title to ownership.

PROPERTY RIGHTS IN DEBT AND CONTRACTS.

A few general reflections on enforcing collection of debt are here submitted. Each organized society, government, commonwealth or association will doubtless in the future continue to protect contracts and rights of property in things; but necessarily with increased and more fully defined limitations. These will be prescribed in proportion as principles of equity, equal freedom and the great law of utility (the greater good, or lesser evil), become understood and applied.

It is not longer possible in enlightened or in really civilized nations to enforce the claim of property in the person other than in one's self. The barbaric fiction of contract under which negro slavery was maintained in this country for two centuries, despite our Declaration of Independence and national Constitution, that negroes were persons from whom "service was due" exists no longer. Under the ancient Greek and Roman law the creditor had power of life and death over the defalting debtor, and over his family and descendents. But however advantageous such a system or rule may seem in the opinion of some who think "a contract is a contract," notwithstanding the unequal relation of the contracting parties, such practice has been relegated to pre-medieval history by our social and industrial evolution, and so is "past praying for." The tendency in all civilized society is to the abolition of "imprisonment for debt." Yet it is difficult to see how the forcible collection of debt can be made effectual without endangering the personal liberty and even life of the debtor, and loss of home to family and children.

Now if government, society or comradeship is bound to enforce contracts such enforcement must in justice be confined to such contracts as are proved to be equitable and consistent with the common good. Gambling debts are no longer legally enforced, save in a few countries, like Turkey or Mexico, where the aim is to make slaves or peons. Contracts, where the animus as well as operation, is to enslave the social unit, or disrupt the social structure, of whatever kind, can have no valid claim for defendment under any rational rule.

I should have a poor opinion of philosophic Anarchism, indeed, if it should propose to enforce such barbarities under the pretense of protecting property rights in debts. If a man were held up by highwaymen, and to save his life or some esteemed treasure, should give them his promissory note, and when out of duress should voluntarily pay it, comrades might not deem it necessary to interfere. But in case he refused to pay it, would they aid the highwaymen to collect it by force, simply because the circumstances in making were not to be inquired into? Yet are not existing contracts often made under conditions just as incompatible with equal freedom? We need not instance those contracts, which are made to capture, wreck and destroy corporate property by trade conspiracies.

Would I justify theft? By no means. There is no necessary relation between theft and the repudiation of a debt. And by no legal casuistry can a failure to pay one be converted into a tort, much less a larceny, since failure is not inconsistent with the strictest honesty, as our periodic panics often demonstrate. Contract values often shrink one-half or more in a single season. Neither debtor nor government can make good the loss. And why should they if they could?

Really what has society, governments or juries to do with maintaining the values of property once exchanged? A buys a horse of B and pays him a hundred dollars in a promissory note. B has the same opportunity to ascertain the value of the note that A has to ascertain the value of the horse. Where no fraud or misrepresentation has been employed, why should A or B call on C, D and the rest of the societary alphabet to keep good the value of the note or of the horse? The one may depreciate as well as the other, or become worthless altogether.

Is not the question one of utility, rather? Under what rule will the incurring of profitless debts and their unavoidable or purposed repudiation, the evils requiring correction, be reduced to a minimum? That is really the only practical question which affects the general weal. Undoubtedly, by leaving the individual free to fix the value of his own credit, keeping it at par by prompt payment, or reducing it to zero by neglect, unwise and uncollectable debts would vastly diminish, and that would prove the best security possible for the straight business creditor, and the best protection for the necessitous debtor. Legal enforcement tends to increase both the formation and repudiation of speculative indebtedness, as all business experience shows. The public good requires that all civil interference in the matter should be withdrawn. Equity under equal freedom cannot be invoked, where the relations of contracting parties are unequal, or where the purpose of either has been to obtain an unequal advantage, or imperil the social welfare.

Even while our laws for collecting debts continue, we may rightly object to having them enforced under usurious contracts. Neither equity nor utility have the least consideration if the value rendered by the creditor is returned to him in installments every ten or twelve years, and still the original claim remains undiminished to the end of time. Laws are not the cause of usury or of other trade vices; they provide only the legal power by which these vices are made promotive of ruin and impoverishment to the unwary and helpless victims of covetous, shrewd and unscrupulous Shylocks. Repeal might not eradicate wholly the vice of contracting debts impossible of equitable discharge, but it would take from such transactions the social sanction and encouragement they now thrive under, and greatly reduce the extent of their mischievous operation in creating individual dependence, involuntary idleness and social demoralization.

BOOKS AND PAMPHLETS

BY J. K. INGALLS,

Sent Postage Paid on Receipt of Price.

REMINISCENCES OF AN OCTOGEMARIAN, 208 pp., Stiff Linen
    Covers, with portrait, - - - - - 40c.
    Paper Covers, - - - - - 25c.
SOCIAL WEALTH, 320 pp., Silk Cloth, - - - 65c.
ECONOMIC EQUITIES, Paper, - - - - 15c.
LAND AND LABOR - - - - - 5c.
PERIODICAL BUSINESS CRISES, before the House Committee
    on Labor, - - - - - - 5c.
    Before Senate Committee on Labor and Education, 3c.
WORK AND WEALTH, - - - - - 10c.
HENRY GEORGE EXAMINED, - - - - 5c.
THE UNREVEALED RELIGION, - - - - 10c.

PRESS NOTICES OF SOCIAL WEALTH.

This handsome octavo volume of 320 pages treats of the usurpations of Capitalism, showing that Land and Labor are the only natural capital, or source of wealth ; exposing the tricks of treating variable and invariable values as one, and explaining the true *mean* of value in Exchange; showing that in the production of wealth cooperation always exists, and exposing the fraudulent methods by which equitable division is defeated.— *Liberty.*

A work of inestimable value in the new field of thought. *World.*

Evinces wide erudition and deep thought.— *Yates County Chronicle.*

Shows a complete mastery of the subject.— *Sociologist.*

Embodies the most advanced ideas of economics. *Washington Post.*

Address,

J. K. INGALLS,
GLENORA. YATES COUNTY, N. Y.

www.ingramcontent.com/pod-product-compliance
Lightning Source LLC
Chambersburg PA
CBHW030827270326
41928CB00007B/932